Praise for *Effortless Entrepreneur*

"Read this book, read, read. You want to be a champion? Get a start from two of 'the Greatest.'"

—George Foreman

"If you want to unlock the simple secrets of success and happiness, then Nick and Omar's easy-to-follow principles are for you."

—H. Wayne Huizenga, owner, the Miami Dolphins; founder, Waste management Inc.; chairman, Huizenga Holdings, Inc.

"For anyone who has an interest in learning how to build and develop a high-performing, fun, and exciting culture, this is a requisite read! I laughed and I learned at the same time . . ."

—Ann Rhoades, president, People Ink and cofounder, JetBlue Airways

"Irreverent, informative, and on target. If you're looking for the real deal on how bootstrap entrepreneurs make things happen, then *Effortless Entrepreneur* is a book for you."

—Jim McCann, founder and CEO, 1-800-Flowers.com

San Diego Christian College
2100 Greenfield Drive
El Cajon, CA 92019

658.11
F911e

EFFORTLESS ENTREPRENEUR

WORK SMART, PLAY HARD, MAKE MILLIONS

By Nick Friedman and Omar Soliman

with Daylle Deanna Schwartz

THREE RIVERS PRESS · NEW YORK

Copyright © 2010 by Nick Friedman, Omar Soliman and Daylle Deanna Schwartz

All rights reserved.

Published in the United States by Three Rivers Press, an imprint of
the Crown Publishing Group, a division of Random House, Inc., New York.
www.crownpublishing.com

Three Rivers Press and the Tugboat design are registered trademarks
of Random House, Inc.

Library of Congress Cataloging-in-Publication Data
Friedman, Nick.
Effortless entrepreneur : work smart, play hard, make millions / by Nick Friedman and
Omar Soliman ; with Daylle Deanna Schwartz. —1st pbk. ed.
p. cm.
1. Entrepreneurship. I. Soliman, Omar. II. Schwartz, Daylle Deanna. III.Title.
HB615.F75 2010
658.1'1—dc22
2010002422

ISBN 978-0-307-58799-2

Printed in the United States of America

Design by Leonard W. Henderson

1 3 5 7 9 10 8 6 4 2

First Edition

This book is dedicated to all current and future entrepreneurs who are taking the time to learn what it means to be an Effortless Entrepreneur.

We hope it will bring you the kind of fulfillment we've experienced by embarking on an entrepreneurial journey that tests your will and passion.

The fact that you're reading this book means that you have already taken a major step in the right direction. We're sure you realize that growing a business takes dedication and commitment. But, the experience of creating a living, systemized business can be so rewarding that it seems effortless. If you follow the strategies in this book, your business and life can begin to run smoothly and efficiently, allowing you to make money and have fun, too!

CONTENTS

Contents

FOREWORD

By Michael E. Gerber, entrepreneur
and founder of E-Myth Worldwide

The hunks in this book are hunks in more ways than the obvious one.

They are hunks who, if you have ever met them, would dazzle you with their enthusiasm, with their energy, with their desire to grow, with their belief in what they do.

They are true entrepreneurs.

But they are more than that.

They are consumed by the opportunity they have taken on to turn the very ordinary—picking up your trash—into the most extraordinary. They created an enterprise out of it.

They are not your twenty-first century tech guys. They are more historically your true twentieth-century "dreck" guys.

Yes, they are young, but the business they have chosen to master is as old as your junk and your trash is.

And, the only way to deal with junk is about as fundamental as mowing your lawn . . . somebody with big muscles has got to do it. And then, once picked up, they've got to get rid of it. Isn't it wonderful that somebody has taken that on? That somebody has figured out how to make money doing what none of us want to do for ourselves? Isn't it wonderfully satisfying to know that by simply picking up the phone, you can avoid picking up your old couch?

How simple can entrepreneurship be than to recognize the pain a large number of prospective customers experience and then ridding them of it?

In this book, you will find out how Nick Friedman and Omar Soliman rose to the challenge and then grew far, far beyond it.

I just love great stories like this one.

Because they tell you how to do the very same thing.

They serve as a world-class exemplar for transforming the ordinary into the extraordinary.

They tell you that despite the attraction that Web applications have for new and emerging entrepreneurs, there are countless more grounded opportunities for each and every one of us to pursue.

Just look around you, as these two guys did.

Look at where people live. Look at what people need to do. Look at how those needs are being satisfied. Ask yourself the question, how would I do that for them instead?

And, lo and behold, the world will open up for you.

I just loved this book.

You will too.

EFFORTLESS ENTREPRENEUR

INTRODUCTION

We were about to be thrown into a shark tank on national television. Our knees were shaking, our palms were sweaty, and our mouths were dry.

Of course, it wasn't a literal shark tank (or we probably wouldn't be here to write about it). We were about to make our debut on ABC's *Shark Tank*, a show that features entrepreneurs pitching their business concepts to a ruthless panel of multi-millionaire investors—the "Sharks"—to present the concept for College Foxes Packing Boxes, a sister company for our successful business, College Hunks Hauling Junk. The Sharks would consider investing in it.

But even if they weren't literal sharks, that doesn't mean facing them wasn't daunting. After all, it was hard to believe we were even there. Just three years earlier we'd been two buddies fresh off four years of partying our way through college. We were working in corporate jobs, with no business experience to speak of. If you'd told our friends then that in three years we'd be on national TV pitching a million-dollar business to high-level investors, they'd have laughed in your face.

"Nick and Omar! You guys are up in five!" a production assistant yelled as a swarm of girls with clipboards and headsets surrounded us, and we were whisked to the waiting room. We'd never thought hauling trash out of a beat-up cargo van would lead us to

Hollywood. But there we were, in the same studio where *Seinfeld* was taped! The elevator doors opened, and we walked on set as five business moguls stared us down with icy glares that would make Medusa freeze. We'd rehearsed our pitch over and over, but before Omar could even finish his first sentence, they threw questions at us like battle-axes.

The name *Shark Tank* was fitting—we were on their turf, being attacked from all sides, scrambling to defend ourselves. We tried to hold our own, going back and forth for what seemed like hours, countering their objections and plugging the holes they tried to poke in our business model. They tried everything from flattery to outright insults to soften us up so we'd agree to their terms. One of the Sharks even called us "pigs," saying we were greedy about how much we asked for in our new business pitch.

Finally one offered us a quarter of a million dollars, which, since College Foxes Packing Boxes wasn't even operational yet, was nothing to sneeze at. It sounded good—until we heard the terms of ownership he proposed. Not only would he take a chunk of the new business; he also wanted a piece of our existing business, College Hunks Hauling Junk!

We had just minutes to consider the offer. Even with a successful business, we weren't so rich that a quarter of a million dollars in our pocket didn't sound nice. We thought about it. We stared around the impressive studio and the ring of ruthless millionaires waiting for our answer. We looked at each other, nodded, stared right back at the sharks, and smiled.

And then we declined.

How could two buddies just three years out of college walk away from a quarter of a million dollars with smiles on our faces?

It's not that we were born rich or had no use for the money; every dollar we had was hard-earned, and our business was our livelihood. We aren't geniuses—just ask any of our teachers from college or high school—and we definitely don't have high-powered degrees. At the end of the day, we're about as normal as it gets.

But we have a great business. Not just in terms of growth, although we've done very well on that front. Not just because it's a business that reflects our values, which treats employees with respect and deals with clients with integrity, although our business does all of those things. No, the reason we could decline that offer with such confidence was because running our business is just way too much *fun*.

From the first moment we broke out of our cubicles three years ago and set out to haul junk, even before we'd earned a single dollar, we felt a sense of freedom, possibility, and control over our own lives that we'd never had before. And it only got better from there. As we expanded and built systems that allowed our company to function more effectively, we discovered that we could spend less and less time doing the everyday grunt work like hauling trash, and more time doing the things we really enjoyed: thinking up new ways to make our company more fun for our employees and having fun with our team members and clients, solving business challenges that truly stimulated us intellectually, and, of course, enjoying our hard-earned rewards. Confucius said that if you find a job you love, you'll never work a day in your life. Well, we took it one step further: We *made* the job we love, and now it's so much fun it seems effortless.

So why would we give up any of that to some investor, just for a quick buck? We're confident we'll make the money anyway, but even if we don't, we're living the lives we've always dreamed of having—the lives of effortless entrepreneurs.

And the best part is that you can do what we did, no matter who you are. We're here to tell you how. We wrote this book so you can see that it's not only possible to start your own business; it's possible to do so in a way that will make your life easier, more fun, and more rewarding than it's ever been. If we could do it, you can too!

Whether you're still in school, recently graduated, disgusted with years in the workforce, or retiring with the hope of making a long-held dream come true, *Effortless Entrepreneur* gives you tools for having the best shot to take control of your own destiny, start a business, and then systematize it so you can spend your days doing the work you *want* to do, not just work you *have* to do. If you've ever considered striking out on your own to become a business owner, this is the book for you.

CHAPTER 1

FROM A VAN TO AN EMPIRE
Nurturing Our Inner Entrepreneur

I t's hard to recall how our entrepreneurial spirit first began. We met in tenth grade and quickly became best friends. At the time, we didn't realize we shared an entrepreneurial nature—formal schooling stifled it, and taking an entrepreneurial approach to our activities got us reprimanded. School taught us that fitting in was safer, requiring us to stay in line, defining us by our classes and grades, and weeding out any behavior considered disobedient. A perfect example was when a math teacher sent a scathing letter to Omar's soon-to-be-angry parents, which said:

> Omar spends all of class speaking with the people next to him. He does not own the correct calculator for the class, and I am not sure if he even owns the textbook. Omar is currently failing this course.

Back then, nobody realized that our "misbehavior" and "bad grades" were really just our entrepreneurial spirit at work. Entrepreneurial qualities tend to be misunderstood. Entrepreneurs typically don't like to adhere to many rules or follow others, and this individuality isn't valued in school. Yet once you've left the boundaries of the system, positioning yourself outside the traditional path helps you make money as a business leader. If high school had been run the way an entrepreneur runs a business, Omar might have been spared some trips to detention. Nine years later, his entrepreneurial perspective provided a new interpretation of what the math teacher meant in her letter:

> Omar spends all of class time networking. He opted not to invest in the $150 graphing calculator, since it would be obsolete upon completion of the course. He was also able to leverage the partnership of neighboring classmates and share the textbook rather than purchase a new one. Omar is currently in the red for this course, but it does not fall in line with his overall vision of growth, so it will probably be dropped from his portfolio.

Doesn't that sound better? Our nature kept us from fully adhering to school rules, which led us into quite a bit of trouble with teachers and administrators. Many kids with our personalities are prescribed medication. Always wanting to stand out from the crowd, we did things to entertain and gain peer approval and attention. Nick took school slightly more seriously than Omar, but he bucked his share of rules too. He always strove to do the least amount of work necessary to get good grades and to finish everything quickly so he could enjoy himself.

That isn't to say there are no benefits to schoolwork. Despite our issues with the system, there's absolutely no way we'd be as successful as we are now without having had the academic education, training, and discipline we received in school. It may not have been appreciated back then, but we're grateful for the teachers and administrators who pushed us to get an education. Entrepreneurs need to take risks and be independent and true to themselves, but they should also always try to learn as much as possible to stay on top of their game and keep their business growing.

BONDING AS PARTNERS

Our first taste of working together to lead others was when our high school football team played our big rival on their turf and won. Though teachers had warned us against rushing the field, as seniors we felt entitled to our moment of glory, so Nick spread the word that everyone should rush the field anyway to celebrate. We hopped the fence, and the rest of our school followed us. As we ran past the losing team, an angry player chased Omar and dragged him down. Nick ran to help and wound up getting kicked in the face by an opposing player's football cleats. So by celebrating, Nick wound up in the emergency room getting stitches. Besides sustaining injury and embarrassment, he was reprimanded for disobeying the rules.

That night we had taken a risk, breaking the rules to lead others for a chance at fun and glory. Of course, that risk backfired and quickly turned into a bad night. That can happen in business too. There are no guarantees that a risk won't backfire. But if you want to break the mold and win glory, risks must be taken and rules must be broken. Staying on a safe path with everyone else leaves no room for change, and life can become boring and meaningless. Even though that risk backfired, we're not sorry we took it. If we hadn't run onto the field, we might not have bonded as friends or seen our ability to inspire and lead a crowd. Even risks that don't pan out can be valuable learning experiences.

Developing a successful business is akin to getting out of the stands and onto the playing field. Parents, teachers, and the school system warn kids not to take risks. As you get older, family and social pressures make you feel stuck in a job. Starting a business can be risky. Staying safe and secure is hyped. If you take a risk, there's a chance you'll get kicked in the head, as Nick was. But you know what? Even getting kicked wasn't the end of the world—we both turned out fine, and went on to be successful. You shouldn't let fear of failure stop you from taking a risk to follow your dreams. No matter what your age, it's never too late to get out of the stands and onto the playing field. Our expectations of running onto the field were significantly different from the results. But tolerance for risk is what helps you become a successful entrepreneur.

During our school years, adults couldn't stop us from taking actions that backfired, and some people even wondered if we'd make it out of high school in one piece. But because we were willing to take risks and weren't afraid of failure, we were able to begin a million-dollar business—College Hunks Hauling Junk—when we were only twenty-two and were named the Youngest Franchisors in America by the International Franchise Association. We were also finalists for the Ernst & Young Entrepreneur of the Year award and were named two of *Inc.* magazine's Top 30 Entrepreneurs in America Under 30 in 2008. Today the company is quickly expanding into cities across the country; we continue to take risks, as our company continues to grow. That's why we encourage you to get out of the stands and onto the playing field to pursue your own business dream.

REAL-LIFE EDUCATION

Growing up, we understood business only vaguely. It was always drilled into our heads that we needed to study hard and get good grades in order to get a good job. But we couldn't relate to that. The great American Dream that we pictured and saw on TV seemed like pure freedom—traveling, owning houses, vacationing, partying, attending sporting events, driving luxury cars, and cruising in boats. It seemed to contradict the get-good-grades, get-a-good-job mentality. How could you enjoy pure freedom if you worked your entire life? We worried that having a job would make us feel trapped. Being constrained by a boss' rules didn't seem like freedom. Boredom and dissatisfaction with following a predetermined path motivated us to change direction.

People assume that studying hard and getting good grades leads to a secure job, but that's not necessarily the case. Education provides a skill set. It's up to you to apply it in real life. If you're in school simply to get a job when you graduate, get ready to be disappointed as you lose control of your own destiny. There's nothing wrong with that if it's what you truly want. But if you're in school so you can get *out* of the system, study hard to educate yourself about the outside world. We quickly realized that to get what we really wanted out of life, we couldn't follow a traditional path.

That conflict between taking a traditional path and enjoying our lives really took shape in our college years. Nick played on the basketball team at Pomona College in California and did as little as possible to get good grades, turning "doing the bare minimum" into a true art form. Study habits developed in high school prepared Nick to optimize his time so he could pursue more fun activities, like a spur-of-the-moment road trip to Vegas. Sometimes he'd drive to Tijuana with a group of friends at night, return at 6 A.M., and go to 9 A.M. basketball practice. Nick structured his class schedule to suit his needs, taking some easy A's that required minimal work.

Omar attended the University of Miami and pursued a different type of Ph.D. than his father had. His stood for "Partying, Hollering, and Drinking." Most of his energy was spent in South Beach, hollering at girls and drinking beer. In his spare time he managed to attend business management classes and learned about marketing, management, and sales. Omar's free spirit made it hard to follow his elders' advice to study hard and get good grades with the goal of getting a good job. In fact, Omar pursued his Ph.D. so hard that his pledge class single-handedly brought his fraternity from the highest- to the lowest-rated on campus.

We both had the same priority: Do as little work as possible. Fun was our goal, and we did a very good job of reaching it!

We poured our energy into cutting corners on work so we could enjoy ourselves. There was always a clash between partying and enjoying school, and settling down to get good grades and "grow up." We struggled to determine when to flip the switch from being a child to being a grown-up with responsibilities.

But what we eventually realized is that you "grow up" as soon as you decide to follow the norm and stop taking risks. The best part of being an entrepreneur is that you never have to grow up. Your childhood imagination, creativity, and daring aren't quashed in an office or a cubicle or by someone else's rules. You're the creator of your own rules and destiny. The world is your catalog. You just need to decide what you want.

Our company didn't evolve from traditional thinking. People do stupid things when they're bored—breaking laws, stretching limits, and other ill-advised activities that can get them into trouble. Channeling restless energy into a powerfully productive endeavor, as we did with our business, is more satisfying. Our school friends are probably the most surprised that, with our priorities, we built such a successful business. They don't understand that for us, working on the business is so much fun that it feels as effortless as partying.

THE JUNK ALTERNATIVE SUMMER

The summer of 2003 was our last before graduating. In previous years, we did what many college guys do—chased girls, partied, and went to the beach. But the one before senior year was different. Nick secured an internship at the International Monetary

Fund. It looked good on a résumé, paid well, and gave him a glimpse into the inner workings of a billion-dollar operation. It was also boring. Omar didn't even want an internship or typical job for college kids. Everyone advised him to build his résumé for after college. But he wanted to try something different and knew he'd never want to work for someone else in the future. So why start now?

We saw that summer as our last with some freedom. Omar was determined not to spend it indoors at a boring desk job. His free spirit pushed for more. Nick agreed, but stayed the course he'd been taught and plugged away at his internship while Omar tried to find a way to make money, appease his parents, and have plenty of time to party. He had to try something on his own; otherwise, he'd end up working at his mom's furniture store, helping to move armoires or assemble complicated modern furniture that came with Swedish instructions. That thought made him shudder.

Then Omar remembered that his mom's customers asked the delivery guys to take away boxes and old furniture. Why not start a junk-removal company with his mom's beat-up cargo van that was used for deliveries? We had no idea exactly what junk removal was, but saw pickup trucks with names like "John's Hauling" on them. That night, we sat down and tried out names to find one catchy enough to attract customers. Suddenly a lightning bolt hit Omar, and College Hunks Hauling Junk was born. Our friends busted out laughing when he said the name. Then we looked at each other and said, "That's not a bad name." The next day Omar printed flyers from his computer:

COLLEGE HUNKS HAULING JUNK
JUNK REMOVAL
ATTIC/BASEMENT/GARAGE CLEAN-OUTS
MISC. MOVING

He began putting them on houses. When he got home he plopped down and forgot about it until his cell phone rang. A voice asked, "Is this the College Hunks? We have junk and need your help!" Omar called Nick, who suggested using the IMF's intranet to post advertisements for junk removal. Since the people who worked there moved a lot, they might need Omar's services. After the ads were posted, calls streamed in steadily. Omar enlisted the help of jobless friends. Nick assisted on weekends. Our operation was far from professional. The van was falling apart, with a poor excuse for brakes. We had no idea how much to charge customers and made things up off the top of our heads.

One time we lined up a job to move two three-hundred-pound, cast-iron radiators up an outside stairway at a house on a hill, nearly thirty steps up. Our friends wouldn't do the job. Omar had a half-hour to dig up four guys to help. He recruited local parking jockeys—guys who got people parking spots, washed cars, and did various odd jobs. Omar piled these characters into the van, including "Sideshow Bob" (his hair resembled that of a character in *The Simpsons*) and "Jailed-Up Rob" (he was often incarcerated). Our crew was far from the college hunks that our name promised.

They were exhausted, covered in sweat, as they grappled with the radiator on the stairs. The dolly's wheels broke on the last step, sending it skidding down the stairs like a sled. The radiator broke, and slammed into the side of the van, leaving a gigantic dent. It was like something out of the *Three Stooges*. The spectacle had people laughing and staring openmouthed at the farce. The client was furious and we had to pay for repairs. Yet, despite the ragtag operation and inconsistent initial performance, our phones continued to ring, and money flowed in.

We noticed that customers placed a premium on having friendly, clean-cut college students in their homes, so we began changing our focus to exceeding the expectations and experience of our clients. After two months, Omar had pocketed close to $8,000 (which he spent after just one month back at school since we had yet to discover the importance of saving and investing). That summer we realized our friendship went beyond just partying and having fun. We had the potential to work in partnership to create a profitable business. Something began to creep up from our subconscious to our consciousness. We'd had a real taste of entrepreneurship, and it wouldn't go away.

REDEFINING JUNK REMOVAL

Omar called Nick during their second semester of senior year to tell him about the Rothschild Entrepreneurship Competition, a business-plan competition at the University of Miami. First prize was $10,000, with ten honorable mentions receiving from $500 to $5,000. Omar thought he could get at least $500 by writing a business plan for College Hunks Hauling Junk. The competition, open to undergrad and MBA business students, drew more than 150 entries.

We knew there were thousands of junk haulers already in business. Most were local independent operations, reminiscent of the outfit on *Sanford and Son*. Our vision was different: a fully branded, entirely systemized operation that didn't require our physical efforts to haul the junk. We knew local outfits bought a truck or two and ran back and forth from job sites to dump sites, as Omar had that first summer. They made money laboring from morning to dusk hauling junk. It was hard work, but they were happy to make the money. We, on the other hand, pictured a cleaner, more attractive operation, since people complained about the appearance of junk haulers.

We also saw an opportunity to supply clients with a customer service center that would be available twenty-four hours a day, seven days a week, with same-day service and a higher-quality source of reliable junk haulers. We envisioned a fleet of trucks combining the efforts of multiple people, and leveraging the equity of multiple business owners to work smarter, not harder. We recognized that if Washington, D.C., needed junk removal, other areas must need it too.

Our business plan was designed to sell our high-speed, high-volume, and clean junk-removal system to cities throughout the country. Even with a small profit margin, the volume would be enough that money would pour into ours and our franchisees' bank account. Our system was designed to be a solid source of steady income, as well to deliver a positive and memorable client experience to cities across the country. We'd live happily ever after growing our brand while the local competition worked hard for the rest of their lives, always struggling financially. We determined that the questions to ask when working on a business are:

• Are you building a system or slinging junk?

• Are you working hard or smart?

The goal of a smart business is to stop slinging junk, working long hours doing whatever grunt work is needed. Instead, work to create systems to deliver cash into your pockets and get the inside work done in a systemized way that allows you to manage people who do it. If you just create a good service and try to do it all by yourself, you won't get far. But if you create effective systems to keep the operation running smoothly, things will come naturally, it will be far more fun, and instead of feeling like torture, the work will feel practically effortless. Creating systems to bring in people to do a lot of the work was the foundation of the business plan for College Hunks Hauling Junk.

Omar spent six straight days working on the business plan. While his friends partied, he diligently crunched away. It was the first time he actually enjoyed schoolwork. In fact, it didn't feel like work at all! This was building something from scratch and felt exciting. He realized that the only reason work felt like "work" was because it was boring and unrewarding—when he was doing something he enjoyed, the hours flew by and it felt effortless.

There was still a lot to do, but Omar had to meet Nick and their buddies for spring break the next day. He worked through the night, finished hours before his flight, and dropped the completed business plan at the entrepreneurship office on the way to the airport. Omar returned to learn that out of 150 entries, twenty finalists had been selected. Each had to present his or her plan to alumni judges—CEOs and business owners from across the country. Omar's entry was one of them!

He was extremely nervous before his presentation but blew the judges away with his passion, energy, and vision for the business. After Omar presented, the entire room seemed energized. One of the judges, Bill Hefner, an alumnus who owns large waste-recycling facilities in the Midwest, chased Omar with his card, saying, "I loved the idea and want to go into business with you!" Then Hefner realized he had given Omar a score of only 7 out of 10 for feasibility in real life, shook his head, and thought, I just chased this kid out of the room to do business with him. He changed his score to 9. Omar's business plan for College Hunks Hauling Junk won first place by 1 point, and he got the $10,000.

We believe there's no such thing as luck in business, preferring to subscribe to the theory that luck is when opportunity meets preparation. Things happen for a reason. Hefner changing his mind wasn't luck. He increased Omar's score after reconsidering the validity and worthiness of the business plan and deciding it deserved a higher mark, even at the last minute. If he hadn't, we probably wouldn't have had the confidence to launch our business. Such what-if scenarios happen all the time in business. Since then, Bill Hefner has been a friend and a mentor to us, which is important to have in any start-up.

Omar received an oversized check at a big banquet and proudly kept it perched in the backseat of his car until graduation. He felt on top of the world, since he rarely got positive recognition in school. Usually he got into trouble. People assume that winning the competition was his turning point, and the prize money helped start our business. But Omar hadn't changed that much. A few shopping sprees and outlandish nights in South Beach put a huge dent in the $10K. While Nick spent the last semester interviewing for jobs,

Omar was partying and spending his winnings. Omar once said that we should have called this book *Party Hard and Start a Million-Dollar Business*—it was a joke, but in fact that's what Omar did.

We don't want to imply that it's not important to work at school. It is. But you should also think hard about why you're in school, what you want to do when you get out, and what knowledge and skills you'll need to accomplish it. School is good for learning broad generalist skills—the ability to communicate in writing, speech, dress, and manners—that parents and teachers emphasize are keys to success in business. If Nick hadn't received his level of education and real-world work experience, he could never have brought those financial and organizational tools and self-discipline into running his own business. If Omar had not received institutional spankings from his professors and deans, he'd never have paid attention to what they covered in his classes about marketing, management, and sales. His school sponsored the entrepreneurship competition. Each of us took different skills from our background and education, depending on what we valued. But by working together our strengths and weaknesses complement each other to get things done effectively.

JUMPING INTO REAL LIFE

When we graduated, we were still conditioned by our programming: Get a good job and put your education to good use. So our business plan got shelved. We believed in its credibility but lacked the balls to try it. Now we were officially adults. We considered ourselves freshmen in life, with no idea what to expect. Unlike college, real life had no orientation, structured schedule, or track to follow. Nick made everyone proud by landing a job as an economic analyst for National Economic Research Associates. It seemed like a perfect way to apply his degree in a real-world profession. After seeing the offer letter he thought, Who is bigger than I am? Then financial reality set in.

Nick quickly became disillusioned with his nine-to-five job and felt trapped in the rat race, with no idea how to get out. He crunched numbers to help billionaires save millions and wondered what he could do for himself, missing more flexible days of fun, especially summer vacations. He longed to regain that personal freedom, and he wondered, How will I get rich by grinding away in an office for the rest of my life, only to put money away for retirement? Physically he was at work, but in his mind he took vacations in Europe, owned houses, and developed his own businesses. At work he surfed the Internet looking at franchises for sale. Despite his distractions, he did well at his job. If he could harness that good work ethic into something for himself, he'd have his freedom.

Omar had no idea what to do after college and floated around trying to figure it out. Nick described him as a "jellyfish," someone who just drifts with the current and does nothing unless pushed. Omar wasn't anxious to enter the corporate world and got a break when he was called for jury duty. Luckily, he landed on a three-month grand jury. So he floated along, happily pocketing his per diem and living at home, rent free. A lady Omar met on jury duty had a son who worked at a well-known health-care research company, and Omar got an entry-level position there with a $39,000 salary. Though that wasn't much money to live comfortably in Washington, D.C., the company had a good reputation. Most employees came from top-level schools like Duke and Dartmouth.

Omar noticed the amazing company culture at work and tucked that lesson away for future use. They had fun games, prize drawings, and trips to Jamaica for reaching goals. People were proud to work there and immediately bought into the vision of the company, compared to employees in many other companies. Their number of job applicants was much more than average, yet salaries weren't high. And they recruited the best of the best. Their company stock continued to grow. But even with all that, Omar didn't like being stuck in a salaried position where he wouldn't benefit from their growth.

We both got restless and disillusioned with our jobs fast. Do you remember the first time you received a paycheck that was less than expected? It's sort of like when a big bully takes half your lunch money every day at school. Nick's starting salary at the economic research firm was $50,000, with a $5,000 signing bonus, full benefits, regular reviews, and the potential for a 5 percent raise every six months. He imagined what he could do with that bonus. But instead of $5,000, that bonus was $2,556 after taxes were taken out!

Omar felt the tax bite too. His first encounter with the lunch-money bully had been in high school working at a record shop. He was supposed to get $8 per hour, but after taxes the pay was much less. It made him disgruntled. Omar also noticed that management cared only about the bottom line. Employees were irrelevant, except to get a job done, and this was reflected in the managers' attitudes. They cared only about their paychecks, and watched people steal without reporting it. Profits dwindled. A few years later the company was taken over by another one. Even then Omar recognized that without a culture, a business would fail.

Reality hit us: the government takes its share of your paycheck first. We had to wise up and spend that lunch money before it could be taken. Nick reflected on his potential if he stayed with his company as an employee. With good performance, he could get a 5 percent wage increase every six months. Staying on the career track could earn a promotion to consultant in about two years. Then he could go to graduate school for an advanced degree, incur $100,000 in debt while earning no income, return to make a nice six-figure salary, and pay off the debt. It sounded good until he did the math. What does 5 percent mean? Five percent of $50K is $2,500, or $208 per month. After taxes it's $135. What could he get with that? How much does it cost to go on a date? He'd need more if he got married, had kids, and had to hire a babysitter to go out. More importantly, he didn't feel any emotional satisfaction from this job.

Working in the corporate world seemed futile. We wondered, Why do employers even bother to say what your salary is before taxes? It creates a false expectation. And it seemed odd that a majority of people just accept the system and don't recognize there are strategies to combat the lunch bully. Most employees look for deductions against their income, like getting a home mortgage. Yet that's really the biggest liability to incur. Sure, you can write off interest payments, but when people get a raise or interest rates drop, they buy a bigger house, thereby taking on more debt. True advantages come to business owners, who can expense all legitimate business operating costs before taxes.

The entrepreneurial spirit that drove us to deviate from the norm in school was lit even more by dissatisfaction with the thought of living the corporate life until retirement. It became tougher and tougher to get excited about working in the nine-to-five corporate world, and we hated the thought of being confined in a six-by-six cubicle till we got promoted to an office and then were confined to that. Having experienced a lifestyle full of fun and freedom had spoiled us. Omar had made $10,000 for a business plan he wrote in a week and $8,000 from two months of junk hauling. Now we worked harder for less money and with less freedom. There had to be more to life than working for a corporation until retirement.

We struggled to figure out what to do. Our free spirits began to get crushed as hopelessness set in about finding a satisfying path that gave us freedom and inspired us to feel about life the same way we had before "becoming adults." We longed to feel passionate about work. Then we remembered the summer we hauled junk in a beat-up van before our senior year. We were dirty, sweaty, sleep-deprived—and excited! That ignited us as we sat in our cubicles. We had to take the plunge and do it full-time!

After three months, Omar threw in the towel. Nick also felt the itch. Launching our business opened up a whole new world of excitement and power. Blowing off good corporate jobs to haul junk seemed absurd to everyone but us. But even before we became truly successful, it was the best move we'd ever made. That's when we truly began to live instead of just passing time.

GOOD-BYE CORPORATE WORLD

We revisited the business plan to figure out how to implement it. While it was award-winning, we had no clue about how to actually start our business and even less about how to grow it into the empire we envisioned. It was important to set it up properly to successfully grow College Hunks Hauling Junk into a national company. We learned everything we could about growing a business, since we had no intention of grinding away as junk slingers. Then it was off to the races!

After spending way too much time planning, we sat down, made a checklist with a time line, borrowed money from our parents, created a limited liability corporation (LLC), opened a bank account, and bought our first truck by getting a small-business bank loan. People thought we were crazy to even consider leaving our jobs. Nick heard "You're quitting a $60,000-a-year job to start a junk-hauling company? Are you nuts?" Both of us heard "You can't quit your job! You need a job. What about your résumé?" We thought: Résumé. For what? To get another job that gives incremental raises? We'd rather do it earning what we're worth than take what someone is willing to pay us. We wanted to build a business.

It took people a long time to catch on that we were serious about building College Hunks Hauling Junk. Even after it launched, it was assumed that we'd started it just to build our résumés to get into business school. Go to business school for what? To pay a hundred grand for another degree and take on debt, just to dive headfirst back into the rat race and struggle up a corporate ladder or get a better job that gets taxed before we see a higher salary or bonuses? Then, if we're lucky, we can finally enjoy life after we retire?

No thank you. We had other plans.

BECOMING ENTREPRENEURS

"I want to be a trash man when I graduate from college!"

We'd bet our bank account those words never came out of the mouth of a single college student. They sure never came out of ours. But now we're trash men. Of course, by *trash men* we mean we're Gen Y entrepreneurs in our mid-twenties who understand that trash is cash and transformed a summer gig into a multimillion-dollar business.

When people hear the name College Hunks Hauling Junk, they usually burst out laughing or stare in confusion as we explain the unique concept. We're not typical junk haulers. Our company provides professional, clean-cut teams to dispose of unwanted items from residential and commercial properties. Clients call our toll-free number to schedule appointments for a team to arrive in a shiny orange and green truck. Their trash is disposed of in an environmentally correct way. After hearing our short elevator pitch, people often continue laughing at our catchy name.

The highly marketable brand of our company, along with our detailed operating systems, has allowed us to grow exponentially. After just two years of servicing the Washington, D.C., metro area, our annual sales surpassed $1.2 million, with eight trucks and twenty-five employees working year-round. But we weren't satisfied being a local company. In its third year our company more than tripled to thirty trucks and more than seventy-five employees nationwide. Our vision is to make College Hunks Hauling Junk a respected brand throughout the country. We've determined that the fastest way to expand nationally is by franchising. College Hunks Hauling Junk offices are opening across the country.

DECLARING INDEPENDENCE

Do you remember the first time you had sex, when you wanted it badly but had no hands-on experience or idea what you were doing? Did you make mistakes and fake your way through it? The first few months of operating our new junk-removal company were like that. We had no idea what the heck we were doing. Just like virgins, we acted confident and improvised as we went along, while the person on the other end pretended not to notice how clumsy and amateurish we were. Clients humored us, acting as if they couldn't tell we were new. We fumbled through with no idea about how to properly estimate a job, let alone how to give appropriate customer service. But working in the business and moving junk ourselves enabled us to create standard operating procedures that could be used across the country.

Trying to hire help was tough at first. Many shied away from this kind of work. One guy's first day on the job was removing furniture from a house where a murder had just occurred. We were startled to find police tape around the door, but we went in, since we we'd been hired to do the job. We worked until we noticed blood splatters on the wall and couch. It was creepy! Neighbors said someone had bludgeoned a guy with a baseball bat. Not surprisingly, that employee's first day was also his last. Crazy things happen in business. You must work harder until your staff is solid. You never know what lurks around the corner.

We shared responsibilities, including answering the HQ phone. Nick's dad strongly warned him against leaving his job immediately, so he handled back-office functions from his day-job cubicle while Omar was on the truck with the younger brothers of friends. Nick did what he could at work and went into the storage closet to answer junk-removal calls. The girl in the next cubicle must have thought he was a drug dealer or having an affair or engaging in some other shady activity, since he'd go there whenever his cell phone rang.

It was even riskier when Omar answered the phone, since he usually fielded calls from behind the wheel of the truck. Determined to do whatever was necessary, he answered calls and wrote down appointments in the scheduling binder while driving at high speed on the highway! It was funny when people got frustrated by his erratic driving and called the 800 number to report it. "One of your drivers is weaving on the road and not driving safely," someone would say. "Thanks for letting us know. We want safe drivers and will take care of it," Omar would reply, trying not to weave, or laugh at the absurdity of it. When you first start a business, you do what you gotta do.

The first summer at College Hunks Hauling Junk was hotter than hell, 110 degrees, with stifling humidity. The alarm went off at 5 A.M. Was it Saturday or Thursday? Days blended together. We got up at the crack of dawn and sometimes came home late at night, filthy, exhausted, and smelling like hot garbage—the dump site's odor permeated our clothes. We'd collapse in bed, then wake up to do it all over again. On our way to the dump some early weekend mornings we'd drive by young people pouring out of bars after a night of fun, as we had done in college. We climbed into crawl spaces and attics, rolled hot tubs up steep inclines, hauled concrete . . . and we loved every minute of it! Each morning we'd empty the truck at a local dump that smelled like rotten food and baby diapers, but Omar would just grin and proclaim, "I love the smell of dump site in the morning!" Even if our bodies felt worn down, our spirits were energized, and for the first time we truly felt like we were alive and doing what we wanted to do. But we also knew we couldn't keep it up forever. We needed employees, systems, and to get off the truck, or we'd burn out fast.

Despite our best efforts, we were extremely disorganized at first. It seemed impossible to keep the truck clean. When we got a flat tire, the tow-truck driver saw all the papers and trash lying around the cab and said, "It looks like you have a bunch of money-grubbing clock punchers driving your truck." Yet it had been just us driving it. His observations on the condition of the truck made us try harder to create a better appearance.

Not everything was difficult in those early months. Making

heads turn was easy! Our brand stood out in the waste-management community. There were many funny looks at the dump sites from the staff and other trash-truck drivers as we rolled in with our bright orange-and-green truck, a big college hunk smiling on its side. One of the dump site chicks even took Omar's number. College Hunks Hauling Junk stood out in ways that made people pay attention and motivated us to give people good things to say about us.

TURNING JUNK INTO TREASURE

Three months after starting the business we received our first big break. A *Washington Post* reporter called to do a story on us. She'd seen our signs around town and couldn't believe there was a company called College Hunks Hauling Junk. The cute young reporter spent a day hauling junk with Omar and two employees. One week later a feature article came out about us in the *Washington Post* Metro section.

It was a huge success! People found the story so intriguing that they actually cut it out and showed it to friends and family. This is when we realized how powerful PR can be. Call volume tripled and our one truck couldn't handle all the business. We needed more trucks and more employees. This was no longer a summer trial. A company was born, and we needed to figure out how the hell to run it. Slowly, we did!

About a year into the business we had to step up our game. Getting a professional 800 number was necessary to take the company nationwide. We tried many number combinations, but most that we liked went to phone-sex operators, and the owners wouldn't sell the number. Finally, we tried 1-800-Junk-USA. It called a doctor's office. Omar asked if they'd sell it. They were hesitant. Patients had used the number for years. We offered $10,000. They declined, since it would cost $3,000 to change their printed material. Before we'd even reached a profit as a company, Omar struck a deal for $13,500. But purchasing 1-800-Junk-USA one year into the business completed our brand and made us a professional, national company, though at the time we only had one location. Once it was ours, any doubts about us growing into a national company vanished. We began to come up with a system to franchise our company.

The business grossed $500,000 in its first year of operation, and we felt like we were walking on water. We had heard about the Entrepreneurs' Organization. Its membership minimum was $1 million in sales. We wanted to join, but that had seemed like a goal that would take years to reach. Our company hit the $1 million mark in our second year! We were not long out of school, but had a profitable company that was growing in ways many people just dream about. Nick's dad finally recognized our passion and energy and gave Nick his approval to quit his day job. People began to take us seriously, and friends stopped questioning our long-term motives. They were clear now!

We decided to get a company car that would present a more corporate image at times when we transported clients and prospective franchisees. After a long day of hauling junk with our team, Omar entered a Range Rover dealership, wearing boots, dirty jeans, and a sweaty shirt. No one even looked at him, probably assuming he was a maintenance guy. He brazenly approached a salesman on the showcase floor, pointed to the shiny white Range Rover beside him, and said, "I'll take that one." Needless to say, some people at the dealership that day learned not to judge a book by its cover.

The first day out in the new car, Omar was challenged. While driving through Georgetown en route to a client meeting, some jerk yelled, "Hey, nice Range Rover! Did Daddy buy that for you?!" Unfortunately, Omar didn't have time to stop and explain to the guy not only that he'd purchased the car, but that he'd bought it for nearly 50 percent less than the jerk could have purchased it for. Instead of a personal purchase, it was a business expense, purchased with pretax dollars. The jerk could buy such a car only by taking on a significantly greater liability.

We were excited knowing that we'd tested the theories we'd discussed while we still worked in the corporate world, and they'd passed muster. It was advantageous to own a business. Those theories had motivated us to renounce the traditional path we'd been taught—working to get ahead in the corporate world—to start College Hunks Hauling Junk. We were living our dream!

MOVING FORWARD

We had the benefit of being able to read good books. From there, we put together our own effective strategies and systems. This book is filled with lessons accumulated on the road to becoming the youngest franchisors in America. Since we've been out of college only a few years, our take reflects entering the world of business after growing up with the new technology most businesses must integrate into their systems. Being part of Generation Y, we work hard but also recognize the importance of having a life that includes fun, friends, and family. We still like to party, but balance has become our goal, along with a serious intention to build our business to reach its highest potential.

Most people who write books about their businesses are much older than we are and speak from a perspective of many years. They've been successful for years and have to look back far to explain how they got there. As entrepreneurs in our mid-twenties, we speak from the vantage point of being in the middle of the fire. As much as we've already accomplished, we're still learning more each and every day. In our short time as entrepreneurs, we've reached a decent level of success, but are leaps and bounds away from where we plan to go. And we have no plans to stop. The lessons in this book aren't just theory—we apply them every single day to turn our own personal and professional dreams into reality.

CHAPTER 2

TEN BUSINESS COMMANDMENTS FOR THE TWENTY-FIRST-CENTURY ENTREPRENEUR

Many people use the Bible to help guide them through life. But even people who strongly believe in the Bible's message and strive to live according to what it says can have trouble remembering every little lesson or rule. That's why the Ten Commandments come in handy. They're meant to be the big fundamental rules that everyone should remember, even when life seems overwhelming, chaotic, and confusing. We might not remember every little guiding principle, but "Thou shalt not kill" stands out in our mind.

The same thing is true in business. So much is happening, and there is so much that an entrepreneur has to learn along the way, that keeping track of it all can get very confusing. That's why we developed the College Hunks Hauling Junk Constitution, with Ten Business Commandments that serve the same purpose for business owners. These are the things every entrepreneur should always try to remember.

Our commandments are guidelines to live by for our business. To this day, every important decision we make still goes through the Ten Business Commandments washer. If it comes out clean on the other end, we consider it a viable option. Throughout the book we'll refer to these commandments as they relate to specific topics. Use them as guidelines for making your own business decisions.

First Business Commandment: *Never sacrifice health, family, or friendships for business reasons.*

Everyone should sign off on this commandment before embarking on the wild voyage of entrepreneurship. It's important to accept that your life shouldn't be defined by what you do or how much money you accumulate. Our culture puts jobs on such a high pedestal that people become obsessive about work. Americans often live to work. On the other side of the pond, Europeans work to live. They have a much less stressful life by putting their emotional well-being first.

Longer vacations, shorter hours, and even midday siestas are important factors in the worklife of many European countries. Of course you'll have long hours and tumultuous times at first. But if they begin to harm your health or relationships, take a breather and reevaluate your priorities. We learned fast that taking care of our physical and mental health improved our ability to do a better job and operate at peak performance. Coping with stress is a common theme in entrepreneurship.

Throughout our first year, Nick's stress was blatant. He'd wake up during the night full of anxiety about the following day and blow up at Omar over relatively insignificant issues. Vacations were more stressful than relaxing. On a trip to Europe during our first year, Nick got so stressed about being away that he lost a patch of hair! After that, he recognized how detrimental stress was and made a conscious effort to find ways to relax and get better sleep. This led to his being more efficient—and to Omar's not having to duck when he saw Nick coming.

Entrepreneurs tend to stay "on the clock." Most stress comes from what we call "small business–itis"—feeling overwhelmed and inferior to other businesses—usually triggered by financial or operational issues. We're inclined to push ourselves too hard. Sacrifices inevitably must be made to make a business success-ful. We adjusted our schedules to allow for solid productivity *and* a personal life. It's absolutely essential to create balance among work, family, friends, and play to keep from going crazy. After all, we became entrepreneurs to lead the life we'd always dreamed of—and who dreams of a joyless, stressful life, where work comes before happiness?

Second Business Commandment: *Mistakes are problems only if you don't learn from them.*

Thomas Edison said of his failures, "I have not failed. I've just found ten thousand ways that won't work." Don't set mistakes aside and hope they won't happen again. When something fails, we try to discover why, how we can prevent the mistake from being repeated, and anticipate similar issues that could arise.

Mistakes teach us valuable lessons. When we started, we had no idea what we were doing and had to make mistakes to figure out what worked. Our first hauling job was removing a pile of concrete. To land it, Omar quoted the client a minimal charge of $99. The concrete alone cost $150 to dispose of, plus two hours of backbreaking work to load it onto the truck! It was a costly but worthwhile lesson at that early stage. We spent a week crunching numbers to calculate all costs associated with our operations, including having to hire two or three employees who would take twice as long to load the truck as we did. In the end we learned from our mistakes and built a system to avoid repeating them.

Third Business Commandment: *Ideas mean nothing without actions.*

Good ideas are like sneezes. They may temporarily infect or get a rise out of a few people next to you, but in the end, they're just air coming out of your mouth.

How often have you been with friends when a lightbulb went on? "You know what would be a really good idea. . . . ?" Everyone has ideas. They're easy to come up with. It's deciding how to implement them that counts. To succeed as an entrepreneur, be prepared to act on your ideas. Otherwise, you're just another dreamer who wishes and longs and prays to have a business but never gets further than sneezing. The people who turn ideas into reality make the difference in this world.

We attempted many business ideas and ventures, such as a party-promotion company and a T-shirt company. They failed because we weren't passionate about them and so wouldn't risk it all for them. Our efforts were only halfhearted and therefore failed. We weren't sorry. At least we tried and learned valuable lessons from those experiences. Don't get discouraged if one of your ideas fails. Keep trying.

Entrepreneurship requires persistence, with actions. Don't just talk about what you want to do—LIVE IT! If you believe you have a good idea, figure out how to bring it to fruition. Take at least one step. Get a business card with your business name. Register a Web domain with a business e-mail address. Research what you need to make it happen. Write down why your idea has a place among other people's ideas. Show that you don't just talk the talk and are actually passionate enough to walk the walk too. Ideas mean little without concrete actions.

Fourth Business Commandment: *Start with a vision, create a strategic plan, and live by it.*

Most people don't have visions; they have dreams. Like most businesses, ours began as a pipe dream. We needed a clear vision to make it happen. Once you create a plan to take action on your dream, it becomes a vision. Every good business has a strategic plan, which is much different from the business plans you see in school. The first piece of this plan identifies your core values, which becomes a litmus test for why you hire and fire people.

Next, determine your company's purpose. Identify your big vision for twenty years from now. Your plan should then focus on intermediate and short-term goals. What does your brand promise to deliver? Finally, what are the most important metrics or measurements for your company? Figure out what factors are essential to measure to ensure that you're on track with your overall strategy. Identify any roadblocks, and assign accountability to yourself and/or members of your team to bring those priorities to fruition.

Fifth Business Commandment: *Create effective systems to keep your business on track and enable individuals to succeed.*

We often hear a small-business owner say something like

this: "Tommy keeps screwing up orders! He's a bad employee." Or: "I don't know what I'd do if Mary left. I can't run my business without her." Many small-business owners don't understand that people don't fail. It's the system, or the lack of a system, that causes failure. Instead of blaming Tommy, the business owner should ask:

- Why is the system failing for Tommy?
- Is there a script or checklist in place?
- Do I have a training program to teach Tommy how to do his job well?
- How do I evaluate Tommy's performance?
- What incentives does Tommy have to get all orders correct?

A great business system never relies on one single employee. The ideal business can take the least qualified employees and put them in positions to do the most productive work. Often a small-business owner mistakenly hires a second person to perform all the different functions of the business at once, rather than concentrating on defining and perfecting each aspect of the business. At College Hunks Hauling Junk we created separate positions, with manuals and a training process for each one. Even if we had to perform these functions ourselves in the beginning, each was treated as a separate job that someone would eventually step into. And if one employee doesn't uphold the system, then don't just complain and let his mistakes impact your business; have a system in place that allows for the employee to be dealt with swiftly and fairly, which ensures that everything keeps running smoothly, and which incorporates what you learned so it doesn't happen again.

Creating systems is part of the ongoing evolution of a business, which should include embracing the speed at which modern technology is evolving in your overall system so you're not left behind. Every, and we mean every, aspect should be systemized and measured. The ultimate goal to strive for is to be able to leave for a period of time (one year is the true test) and return to find your business more profitable and efficient than before. That reflects a truly systemized business.

Sixth Business Commandment: *Work ON the business from the outside, not IN it.*

A great entrepreneur builds systems to run the business as if it were a machine, and stands over it instead of being part of its inner workings. A business owner should sell that machine to clients and perfect its functionality, but not sit in the gear room. How many times have you seen a local store owner answering phones, doing paperwork, and assisting customers all at once? This business owner works IN the business, not ON it, and hasn't identified the different positions within his business, such as receptionist, salesperson, and cashier. Instead, he does all those jobs himself.

Creating manuals and training maps for each position from the get-go forces you to evaluate what needs to be done and helps identify tasks you might not think of right away. That can mean fewer unpleasant surprises down the road. At first, you'll likely have to work IN your business and do most, if not all, of the work for each position. That's common when you start out. But create a system that allows you to just work ON it as soon as possible. Once that system is operative, a business gains its true value.

There's a difference between being a business owner and being self-employed. If you want a real business, absorb this point. A business owner grows the business. A self-employed person works in the business to generate income. If you own a sandwich shop and make sandwiches all day, you're a sandwich maker working for yourself. If we wanted to be junk slingers, we'd still be on the trucks. But to grow our business, we had to get out of daily operations and focus on developing systems, increasing sales, and evolving our brand.

Seventh Business Commandment: *Develop staff, client, and community loyalty.*

The atmosphere of a business should communicate to staff and potential customers that they've entered a special place. To generate any sort of employee loyalty, a company culture must be created where employees feel smart, valued, and important. This comes from awards, recognition, positive reinforcement, increased responsibility with accountability, and empowering them by making them realize that their opinions matter.

After we fostered the development of our company culture, our team became very effective. Working for us becomes more than "just a job." Many businesses say, "The customer comes first." At College Hunks Hauling Junk, we believe our employees come first. If the people who work at your company are happy, your customers will receive the highest level of service. A company culture is the heartbeat of any organization.

We don't give customer service; we cultivate *client loyalty* by providing an experience clients can't forget. Doing an adequate job gets a mediocre response. Clients may be satisfied, but you'll

be off their minds fast. If your service is impressive, they'll recommend your business and become repeat customers. A catchy
brand gets clients to try your product or service once. A good
experience keeps them coming back for more and makes them
your best salespeople. Because we recognized the importance of
the overall client experience, we have over 40 percent repeat and
referral business in D.C. alone—remarkable for a junk-removal
service.

Your goal shouldn't be to just satisfy your customers' needs.
You want to leave them marveling about the level of service your
company delivered from start to finish. Everyone who has contact
with a client or is involved with providing the service should buy
into these efforts. A loyal client becomes a cheerleader for your
company and wants your company to succeed. Figure out how to
wow the customer at every interaction point. Everything should
make for a superb, unforgettable experience for customers, like
the meal you want to have again and recommend to friends.

Along with creating a loyal staff and customers who are
wowed by your service, it's important to develop loyalty in the
communities you serve. It may sound like a cliché to advise you
to become active in your community, but we strongly recommend
that you find ways to do it. Community involvement can truly
feel like a fun activity instead of seeming like a duty. We help out
whenever we can. Walking into a classroom full of bright-eyed
ninth-graders and seeing them get excited about entrepreneurship is an awesome feeling.

Sponsoring a basketball tournament or a Little League team
can turn an average Saturday afternoon into a fun-filled day. We
also feel good about donating money to a scholarship fund. Look

for opportunities that match your personality, hobbies, and business. If you don't have the time, donate some money to a local charity. If you want the community to use your business and help it grow, then you should help the community grow as well. It's not only good karma—it's good business.

Eighth Business Commandment: *Image is everything.*

College Hunks Hauling Junk began in June of 2005 with one dump truck. We answered the phone as we drove, scribbled appointments in a binder, and, except for a few siblings of friends who could be dragged out of bed, the company staff was just the two of us. But from day one, we projected the image of being a large, national company.

Our demeanor created the appearance of a solid establishment that people could feel comfortable doing business with. Attention to external details goes a long way toward creating the aura of being a reputable business. Our image made people think we were much more than two recent college grads who were flying by the seats of our pants to build the company.

We did what we could, making sure the truck was always clean and the logos were shiny. Our Web site looked cutting-edge. We used an assortment of names on e-mails to create the facade of a staff, giving the impression we were a much bigger company than we were. After just a few months in business, customers often said, "You guys are a national company, right?" To their surprise, we'd answer, "Not yet," as we smiled inside about our national future. They had no idea that behind the scenes we were twenty-two-year-old kids learning as we went along, since from the outside our image was flawless.

Ninth Business Commandment: *Be the best at ONE thing.*

Our initial business plan included offering junk removal, moving services, and labor. We soon realized that it would be impossible to be the best at all these services, so we decided to do only junk removal. The best doctors, professors, music producers, and businesspeople find their niche and master it. A surgeon who performs only one type of surgery is much more sought after than a general one because he has mastered his art.

We made junk removal our niche and learned everything about it. We wanted to be the best junk-removal company and set about accomplishing that. It's imperative to recognize what you can be the best at when you create a business plan and to focus on that ONE thing as you write it. It's tempting to expand to provide services that are an outgrowth of what you start with. But if you expand to offer other services, you don't become as proficient in any as you'd be in just one.

Stick with your forte and perfect it. Put all your energy into figuring out how you can become the best at that ONE thing. Once your business is thriving, you can revisit other ideas and see if you can add another service. In a booming economy, having a niche service or product is ideal because you can dominate that niche. But be mindful if that niche shrinks. Once the junk-removal process reached a consistent level of success, we were able to start diversifying in order to gain a revenue stream from another niche.

Tenth Business Commandment: *There are always people smarter than you—hire them!*

We're the first to say that we're not geniuses. We didn't invent something extraordinary, create a computer program, or master the stock market. We took one of the oldest and simplest concepts and made it a multimillion-dollar company in less than three years. Recognizing your limitations early helps you find ways to strengthen those areas or compensate by hiring the right people.

Some business owners act like know-it-alls. They won't ask for help, believing they're perfect. Know-it-alls won't hire someone who can do something better, since it might make them feel inferior or look bad. That mentality is counterproductive to being a successful entrepreneur. Acknowledging your business weaknesses is smart and allows you to improve your company. Ask the best entrepreneurs in the world and they'll say the same thing: *A key to success is to surround yourself with people who are better than you at things you're not good at.*

If you're disorganized, hire or partner with someone who's organized. If you're detail-oriented but not a big-picture type, hire or partner with a creative visionary. As a business owner, it's imperative to embrace your weaknesses. A business is like a puzzle. You can't put together a big one without seeing where the grooves are. Working with smart people creates fit that holds your puzzle together. If you cannot afford to hire staff, cultivate strong mentors first. Once you clearly identify your vision for the future and develop at least the outline of a solid company culture, good people will be attracted to your vision, your values, and your culture.

CHAPTER 3

GET READY
The Making of an Entrepreneur

Nick learned early how to hustle. When he was ten years old, he was obsessed with basketball and became passionate about collecting autographs. Charles Barkley was his idol. An autograph from him was his holy grail. As a sixth-grader, he attended Washington Bullets games and saw people lined up near the locker rooms to get autographs, but they never got close to the players. With a strong desire to meet Barkley and get his autograph, he devised a plan. The ball boys wore khaki pants and white polos with the Bullets logo and had a badge hanging from their neck. So Nick was prepared when Barkley's team was in town. His dad took him to the game. Nick wore a white polo shirt tucked into his khakis, with his ticket on a shoestring around his neck to resemble a badge. In his pocket was a disposable camera, a pen, and an oversized special edition Charles Barkley trading card. After the game, he casually and confidently approached the basketball court, adrenaline pumping and hands shaking. He picked up a small wastebasket as if he were cleaning up and carried it to the locker room, which was guarded heavily. No one stopped him! He calmly walked in. There was his hero, Charles Barkley. Just then a real ball boy asked what Nick was doing. A security guard led him outside, where he saw team buses in the garage. He slipped into the parking area. Family members and media were waiting, so he saw another chance. Sure enough, Barkley emerged, swarmed by autograph seekers. Nick squeezed his way to the front and held his card and pen up. Barkley signed it. Nick held up his camera to show he wanted a photo. Barkley obliged, and Nick quickly handed someone his camera and jumped into the photo. Success by any means necessary!

From a young age, Omar refused to be kept out of any venue, whether a concert, a nightclub, or a sporting event. No matter how long the line or how difficult it was to get in, he always found a way. One weekend he was with friends at the beach in Maryland. The main beach bar was throwing the biggest party of the year, but stopped letting people in before Omar and his friends got there. So they went around back, found some bags of ice, put them over their shoulders, and walked in the kitchen entrance acting like staff. Once they were in, they joined the party. Omar learned early that with the right demeanor, he could pass for what he needed to get through doors.

In Miami, he'd get friends into celebrity-packed nightclubs by telling the bouncer he'd buy a VIP table for $2,500; once inside the club, he'd tell the waitress it wasn't his scene and he didn't want the table. Since the bouncer was outside, the waitress was unaware of the agreement. Thinking Omar was a big spender, the club would let Omar's party leave the table. He'd always get to stay in the club while everyone else was stuck outside pleading to get in.

At a *Maxim* Super Bowl concert, celebrities were allowed onstage by showing a special stamp on their hand. He drew the stamp on his hand with a ballpoint pen, quickly showed it to the security staff, and next thing he knew he was onstage with Cuba Gooding Jr., Terrell Owens, and tons of other stars. Once Omar set his mind to doing something, he found a way to give himself the image or brand he needed to attain what he wanted.

BECOMING AN ENTREPRENEUR

Those kinds of pranks might sound like troublemaking to some people, but they actually reflected an entrepreneurial spirit. Even having what many considered great career jobs, we couldn't handle the day-to-day grind of working for someone else. Some people prefer what they perceive as security in having a steady job. We saw it as an insecure and stifling way to earn a living and longed for the freedom to create our own destinies in business. You have to decide what feels best for you. People become entrepreneurs for different reasons. Some common ones are:

- They're fed up with their day job.
- They have a desire for more freedom and power.
- They hold a strong belief in their idea.
- They're tired of working hard and not seeing enough fruits of their efforts.
- They want to make a difference in people's lives.

Every entrepreneur is different in how and why he or she takes this path. Some successful business owners and investors follow preexisting and successful systems to create wealth rather than creating their own business from scratch. A franchise is an existing business system that allows someone to benefit from the support and improvements of an established system. You have to take the path that best suits your needs and decide how far to grow it.

Start with a vision, create a strategic plan, and live by it.

Many entrepreneurs see starting a business as bringing fantasies to life. They have a clear picture of the future, write it down, and make it happen. You don't need to figure out how it will happen right away. But you should know it *will* happen and how it will look. That can stoke your fire to take the idea a step or two further by learning necessary skills or whatever your vision requires. When you have a strong belief in the business you're building, it's easier to motivate others to work hard with you. Enthusiasm about your business can be contagious.

For us, JOB is an acronym for just over broke. There's no such thing as job security. Look how many people got laid off during the economic downturn. And what did many of them do? Start their own businesses! People always need goods and services. If you can provide something they want or, better yet, something they need, you can make money in any economy. Owning a business has a lot of advantages, in particular good tax benefits. Everything you buy for your business can be paid using pretax dollars. That saves money and makes buying more fun.

Work ON the business from the outside, not IN it.

When we started, everything was new and exciting. Nick worked on our business from his day job and at home and woke up at 4 A.M. every morning to empty the truck before going to work. This isn't a grind if it feels like fun and is a huge shift from the traditional grind of a day job. When you're building something of your own, even when you're "working" hard, it can feel as effortless as just having fun. But after months of sacrificing sleep and personal time, it can start to feel suffocating. You can become disillusioned if it seems that the routine is too hard or that the venture will never work as planned. There's a moment of truth when you find ways to work smarter, not harder, as we did. We had to work on our business instead of in it, or quit altogether. Fortunately, we persevered and made it to higher ground.

PERSONAL ASSETS

We've identified qualities that are helpful for succeeding as an entrepreneur. If you have them all, you have a leg up. If you don't, do your best to develop some of them. They appear in varying amounts in different individuals, but some combination should be present not only to hatch an idea but also to nurture it to take on its own life. You can work with people who have the skills you're weaker in. Our partnership works because we complement each other's strengths and weaknesses.

Getting a partner or finding good people to work with you can make up for what doesn't come naturally to you. Each of us has some of the necessary entrepreneurial traits, but neither of us was a born entrepreneur who naturally had all the qualities we discuss in this chapter. The trick was recognizing what our strengths were and capitalizing on them, and recognizing our weaknesses and either finding ways to improve on them or making up for them by working with others.

You can develop some entrepreneurial qualities. Keep in mind that you might possess a lot more than you think. We didn't recognize many of our skills at first. Friends and family were doubtful when we began. We'd done a lot of partying and cutting corners to get work done in our day jobs and had no experience running a business, much less building one beyond working out of our parents' houses. Sometimes you have to dig deep to bring out hidden qualities, as we did. We didn't know our strengths until we tried to cultivate them. The desire to start a business can help you develop assets you don't even know you have. Below are some we developed that helped us build our business.

LEADERSHIP

Being a leader is without a doubt the most important skill for a successful entrepreneur to have. It's said that you can lead a horse to water, but you can't make him drink. Well, if water signifies the vision of a business, an entrepreneur must lead his employees to it. How an entrepreneur gets his horses to drink (buy into the vision) makes all the difference. An average leader forces them to drink by establishing authority as "the boss." His horses drink reluctantly. A visionary leader inspires his horses to drink by getting them excited about being part of the process and making them feel important.

When we started, Omar wrestled with leadership. He was a twenty-two-year-old with employees his own age or older and felt he could never be himself and still maintain a professional, bosslike image. Omar is laid-back and fun-loving, but his persona in the early stages was uptight and distant. A visit to Faisal Ansari, our Orlando franchisee, shifted his thinking. When Omar entered the office, Faisal was at his desk with sunglasses on his head, joking with one employee while directing another. His attitude was more like that of a buddy. But the employees respected and listened to him and were there from the beginning. Even more amazing, nobody had quit or been fired!

It hit Omar hard: Being a good leader is about BEING YOURSELF. From then on he didn't TRY to be the boss. He WAS the boss, yet acted like the laid-back, fun-loving guy he is. When he took over running the call center, Omar kept those leadership qualities intact. Our call center boasts extremely low turnover, strong performance, and staff committed to the company vision. While leaders share specific characteristics, they relate to others by being themselves. You can become a *visionary leader* and inspire your staff to work well as part of your team by being conscious of what a good leader does:

- *Sees the direction clearly and communicates it:* If you're unsure of your direction, people won't have confidence in you. When you create a vision plan (more on this in chapter 4) you can be prepared before you try to lead. Confidence in how you communicate instills confidence in those who work with you.

- *Evokes passion and motivates others to see the vision:* Excitement is contagious. When your team feels how much you believe in what you're doing, they're more likely to get onboard with you.
- *Is open to fresh ideas:* A leader isn't a one-way thinker. When your team understands that you listen to their ideas and come in with new ones to try, you come across as more on top of your business than someone who's not flexible.
- *Inspires creative thinking:* Team members who feel that they're truly part of the business and that their ideas are valued are more likely to think creatively. Even if you don't always use their ideas, listen to what your team thinks and show appreciation.
- *Refuses to take personal credit and gives credit to staff:* A good leader doesn't need the glory. Instead, all efforts belong to the team, as does the credit for accomplishments. Your reward is a successful business.
- *Allows people to make mistakes:* Mistakes can teach valuable lessons. They happen. A good leader trusts the team to take responsibility for tasks and doesn't try to do everything him- or herself to ensure that it gets done right. Mistakes are accepted as part of the road to success.
- *Makes sure others, including the front-line employees, see, accept, know, and embrace what to do, and feel good about it:* When you have good systems (more on this in chapter 4) and a company culture (more about this in chapter 7) in place to make

everyone feel like a valued part of the team, it makes people want to follow you.

Visionary leaders share their vision in a way that makes you believe it. Dr. Martin Luther King Jr. was the quintessential visionary leader. He had a dream and painted that picture. We're certainly not saying all entrepreneurs need to be the next Dr. Martin Luther King Jr., but that doesn't mean they can't learn from the ways that the great visionary leaders like him inspire others to share their dreams. In our partnership, Omar is more the visionary. He presents a vision that seems impossible to accomplish and makes it happen. When Omar said he'd write a business plan and win a prize in the competition, it seemed highly unlikely that he would actually win first place, but he won. When he said ours would become a million-dollar business after one year, it sounded like hogwash. Nick tried to be "realistic." But sure enough, we hit $1 million in sales in our second year. Next Omar announced that we'd sell franchises nationwide. It happened! None of these and other things would have materialized if Omar hadn't envisioned them and convinced the rest of us to believe in the power of his vision.

CREATIVITY

An entrepreneur needs an inspired idea. The good news is that ideas are all around you. While it's true that everything under the sun has been invented, you can improve on existing concepts to make them remarkably attractive and marketable. An idea can come from a vision or an observation, or by adapting someone else's. A creative thinker can recognize the possibilities in ideas and develop them in unique ways.

Ideas mean nothing without actions.

Being a creative thinker helps you come up with new products, novel methods, or original approaches to challenges. Entrepreneurs try to stay ahead of the curve and get the market to buy into their ideas or may come up with a unique way to deliver a solution, as TiVo did. We love TiVo and think it's an amazing invention. TiVo's inventors simply recognized that people might never learn how to program their VCR and created an alternative solution. Our creative thinking allowed us to take a traditional business and ramp it up in ways that set it apart from those of our competitors.

The most common complaints from would-be entrepreneurs are "I need an idea" and "I have too many ideas." Complaining about needing an idea is like complaining that you need oxygen. While everything has been invented to some degree, there are millions of opportunities and ideas around you every day. Find a good product or service and make it better. Be creative and pair a need with a product or service that fills it.

If you suffer from the too-many-ideas syndrome, it's hard to keep your attention from jumping around. While it's fine to investigate several potential ventures, stick to those with the strongest legs. Nick has a folder called "Future Business Ventures" that he reviews monthly. Identify which one idea will truly stand out. Even those that seem stupid are worth investigating. A junk-removal company called College Hunks Hauling Junk got strange comments and seemed silly, but look how far it's gotten. Ask yourself, "Why do people need my product or service? Why do they need it now?" If you have no answers, find them before you launch.

Test your idea. We hauled junk during summer vacation. Generating a significant amount of income showed that the idea had weight. It was put to the test when we entered it into the business-plan competition. Winning first prize out of 150 entries proved this idea was worth pursuing. When evaluating your ideas, decide which you're most passionate about and which sound the most fun or exciting. We considered other business ideas but were most passionate about College Hunks Hauling Junk. It had a brand, and we could feel and see it growing. If you're not passionate about your idea, you won't do whatever it takes to make it successful. If things don't go as planned, you'll quit.

Act on your ideas! People often say they thought of something and then someone else did it. So what? Do it anyway! Make it a stronger brand, a superior product, or a better service. Trash-removal companies have been around for ages, but we found a unique way to brand and run our business. There's always room for an old idea with a new or fun twist. Find the hook and make it happen!

PASSION

The movie *Hustle & Flow* illustrates the resolve of an aspiring rap artist named DJay, who, despite having almost nothing, decides to sell his few possessions so he can record a demo and take a chance at really living the life he wants. While his efforts fail, DJay illustrates the power of being passionate about doing what he loves and creating the vision in his mind. It makes the rest of his life seem insignificant in comparison. Passion can be very powerful when used to create something you believe in.

Passion is what fuels an entrepreneur. This doesn't mean you have to be passionate about every aspect of your business or even what your business is based on. DJay's passion for his music kept him going when he couldn't get a record deal. We're not passionate about junk but we are passionate about our business, helping our franchisees achieve their dreams, and creating an environment for our staff that's the opposite of our own corporate experience. We're passionate about making money on our own terms and knowing that the work we put into our company rewards us. Make sure you enjoy what you do, feel some excitement about the business you want to build, and have fun!

There will always be haters and naysayers. That's just life. People may question everything you do, sometimes without meaning to, sometimes out of spite or jealousy. We believed in our vision enough to brush off negative comments and move forward. Use the doubt as a motivation to prove them wrong instead of letting naysayers dampen your vision. We'd have quit before our first truck was acquired had we listened to all the negative comments. Passion kept us going. If you get constructive criticism, listen to it and consider it. Sometimes you'll get valuable insight. It's helpful to find people you respect who can act as mentors. Solid advice, even with negative points, can teach you a lot. But if someone is being stupid, criticizing just to put you or your idea down, view it as more motivation to succeed so she can eat your dust.

FOCUS

You can't ride more than one bicycle at the same time. When we started College Hunks Hauling Junk, we had thousands of business ideas. It took costly distractions to realize that we couldn't do everything. We tried to launch side businesses. Every time we got away from our core, the decision came back to bite us in the butt. The key is figuring out which idea has legs and sticking to it.

Be the best at ONE thing.

That said, many entrepreneurs juggle several balls. Most probably multitask on the go, checking voice mails, eating, or organizing notes as they rush to meetings. But make sure you stay focused. We learned the hard way. Almost everyone says, "You must make lots of money reselling junk." Our business model makes that extremely difficult. The logistics and expenses involved in separating, storing, selling, and transporting items is a different business altogether. Yet we allowed ourselves to be influenced and moved into a 2,500-square-foot warehouse after two years of business. BAD BUSINESS DECISION!

Omar questioned Nick with skepticism before we signed a three-year lease on the warehouse. Nick was sure we could sort items there, resell the junk, and make money on the metal we hauled away. Until then we'd let our teams keep what they found on jobs. Many sold items on eBay and scrapped unwanted metal. Nick took the leap and signed a lease on the warehouse. It doubled our monthly rent and was ten miles from our existing location. Labor costs to sort, store, and sell items skyrocketed. Unfortunately, 90 percent of the items we removed were junk. The rest wasn't worth the time or energy to sort, store, and deliver. We were better off with our previous system.

In addition, team members' morale decreased significantly. They saw it as a greedy decision, since they couldn't keep items they found and their job became twice as difficult. As Omar had feared, our primary business suffered as we tried to create this new stream of income. We were no longer in the junk-removal business and knew nothing about the junk-reselling business. We were stuck in a three-year lease that we had foolishly signed for personally. Those types of decisions can be fatal.

There's no harm in having a side venture as long as it doesn't fully occupy you or distract you from the core business. One useful tool is to get a picture of an owl. Yes, an owl. Put every idea you have on a board with the owl above it. The owl signifies "Who?" Who will do it? If you're busy and can't do something, you'd better know who can carry out that new project. If you don't, it needs to stay on the shelf. Don't even consider additional ventures until your core business is systemized to the point that it can grow profitably without you.

KNOWLEDGE

Never stop learning. We probably didn't read a single book from cover to cover until after college, when our real learning began. Once we found something we were truly passionate about, that we could devote our energies and efforts to, we became sponges, soaking up as much information as possible. We attended seminars, read books, and picked the brains of business owners who'd made it. Once we were actually interested in what we were learning, it stopped feeling like work and became genuinely exciting. It's helpful to have a clear, sharp understanding of basic economics and the principles of marketing and sales to start a successful business. Education helps develop those abilities.

Create effective systems to keep your business on track and enable individuals to succeed.

The biggest frustration with all that information is that it often ends up in a pile of papers or books but is never implemented in the business. We allocate one week a year to pore over our learning pile and assign specific scheduled times to implement new ideas to improve our business. Learn as much as you can about business and your field, and continue to thirst for knowledge to help grow your business. Books can have the highest return on investment. We paid $20 for our first book on how to start a business. It literally changed our life path, providing the backbone for our multimillion-dollar business. That return on investment is so huge that it almost can't be measured.

RISK TAKING

Entrepreneurs often live on the edge. Taking necessary but extreme risks can steer you away from the normal and safe path most people feel secure with. Very successful entrepreneurs are willing to take leaps of faith into uncharted waters. While they have confidence in their ability to survive, they understand that there's a chance they won't make it out. We know that taking risks isn't a sure bet. Far from it. But there are no guarantees that you'll keep your day job or that your marriage won't end in divorce or in most other endeavors. Sometimes you just have to take a chance to make a dream real.

Not every business involves walking a tightrope without a safety net. Good preparation lessens risks. So does having a good team in place—people who are good at doing what you're not so good at. You can slowly build your business while you still have a day job and put money away as a safety net before you go full-time. But even if everything is set up properly, you might have to make quick decisions that don't work out. Then it's up to you to overcome a wrong move so you can keep going and figure out the right ones.

There can easily be less-than-positive outcomes, like when we led our classmates onto the football field and Nick got hurt. If risks had guaranteed good outcomes, everyone would take them, and they wouldn't be risks. Sure, had we not run onto the field, Nick would have avoided the emergency room, but he might have regretted missing the opportunity to celebrate victory and see he was a leader. By taking risks he ensured that, whether he succeeded or failed, he was living a life without regret. Taking risks can put you in a position to achieve greatness: taking the safe and easy way never does. Look at risks as chances to make progress or to learn a good lesson. Either way, they can be positive.

There's a difference between a risk and a gamble. A gamble is a blind-faith leap into the unknown that's made in desperation, without passion. A risk is something you think about and believe in. You consider potential outcomes, then decide to go ahead, despite obstacles and warning signs. It's a leap of faith with a clear vision. Regretting a risk that fails gets in the way of your taking them in the future. Some things are out of your control. You may expand your business at the wrong time, or a corporate entity may exert its power to your detriment. But the truth is, bad things happen whether or not you take risks. Clinging to the "secure" and easy corporate path won't guarantee you a job forever—but it will make it far more difficult to achieve greatness and realize your dreams.

We see risks as opportunities. We wanted a presence on opening day at the new Washington Nationals baseball stadium but couldn't afford the club's advertising rates. But the entire city would be there. President Bush would attend. Security was high. It would be difficult to get close at game time, so we parked our trucks by the stadium the night before. The next day our trucks were towed, but we got them from the pound. The setback didn't deter us from our guerrilla marketing. We decided that Nick should take one truck and circle the stadium to find a place to distribute flyers. Nick saw a roped-off area where people arrived by subway. It was perfect!

Nick pictured our truck strategically positioned, with hoards of people viewing the College Hunks Hauling Junk truck on their way to the game. A D.C. police officer guarded the section. Nick told him, "We're here to pick up trash after the game." The policeman opened up the roped-off area, and Nick drove in, positioning the truck exactly as he'd imagined. Our truck was the first thing people saw as they arrived for opening day! Two hours later, an official realized that we shouldn't be there and alerted the officer who had let us in. He was furious that Nick had lied to him. We apologized profusely, saying that it was a big misunderstanding. But our mission was accomplished. As the saying goes, sometimes it's better to ask for forgiveness than permission, especially for guerrilla marketing.

When you start your business, take a deep breath and try something new. No matter what the outcome, find something good in it. If it works, great! If it doesn't, what did you learn? Write it down and analyze it with your team to figure out how to do it better next time. Don't be afraid to take smart risks. Do what you can to research your decision, prepare for whatever you can, get backup from whomever you can, and try. You have to be *willing* to take risks. That doesn't mean you have to take one. But be willing to consider it. It can lead to great success for your business.

Many people avoid taking risks because they're scared to fail, then wonder why their lives don't improve. Nick likes to say, "Oh welllllll," when things seem to go wrong. No matter how significant the issue, saying those two words somehow puts situations into perspective. When things go well, he says, "Yuuuuup," to celebrate minor victories. It's important to avoid the extreme lows and highs that failing or succeeding can bring. Each can change quickly, so acknowledge what happened, learn any lessons, and continue moving forward.

Failure was not an option for Steve Jobs, who dropped out

of college to sell personal computers he assembled in his garage. That was the beginning of Apple Computers, which revolutionized the computing industry and made Jobs a multi-multimillionaire before he was thirty years old. Passion, not fear, builds a business.

Are you scared to take that big first step? We see this often in prospective franchise owners. Many have never owned a business. We discuss getting past fear with those who seem afraid to take the leap to start their own business or who drag their feet about starting. If it's clear they do want to move forward but their traditional way of thinking holds them back, we ask them to picture the absolute worst-case scenario and then ask how they would rebound or recover. Ask yourself what's the worst that could happen and what you could do if it dies. Is it worse than missing an opportunity to run the business you want? Ask yourself these questions if fear blocks your steps forward. Focus your creativity, vision, passion, and determination to do what seems risky. Stay focused on the endgame. Be at least a little intrepid if you want to succeed!

If you're serious about starting a business, you can learn how to develop these assets in yourself, as we did, just as you accumulate other business assets. Our leadership skills before we began College Hunks Hauling Junk basically amounted to leading friends into trouble. We've done some crazy things for our business because that's who we are. Other people take different routes. Find your own entrepreneurial style, one that you're comfortable with, and work it. If you really want your own business, you CAN do it! Create a plan to make the most of your personal assets and find people who are good at other things to complete the picture of your business. Then build your business one brick at a time.

CHAPTER 4

HUSTLE AND GROW
Creating Your Business Foundation

From the minute we purchased our first shiny dump truck, our intention was to be a national company. Even then we thought big! It was obvious that we wouldn't be happy to be just a major player in the Washington, D.C., area. Our vision was to have our orange-and-green trucks roaming neighborhoods across the country. This mentality impacted every decision we made from the very beginning. Thinking large separates the big boys from amateur businesses. All our decisions and actions reflected our objective of owning a national company. We'd ask ourselves, "How will this work for someone in Chicago or Los Angeles?" even when we were just local. The objective was to provide a service that could work in every city.

WEARING YOUR ENTREPRENEUR CAP

After we watched *Hustle & Flow*, "Hustle and Grow" became one of our company's slogans. We knew that if we *hustled* to work hard and pursued our vision of creating a national brand, we'd continue to *grow*, despite setbacks along the way. This mantra helped prevent us from getting burned out after working consecutive fifteen-hour days. Watching the movie, we were inspired by the protagonist's swagger, drive, and resolve to succeed no matter what. This confidence and desire to use any means necessary to succeed typify the attitude of successful entrepreneurs. We adopted it as our own.

There's a bit of Bart Simpson in all entrepreneurs. We play by our own rules. We have an ego, confidence, and an unwavering drive that's unaffected by authority or rules. Starting a business isn't easy, but it can be done by setting your mind to it and persevering to make it happen. If you can target your market—who will buy your product or use your services—you can hustle to tap into it. Just having a cool idea isn't enough. You need to know whom to market to and how to get their loyalty.

VISION: SETTING SHORT- AND LONG-TERM GOALS

Ideas mean nothing without actions.

Having vision means creating what you want in your mind, then taking actions to make it real. To grow your business, create a vision plan—in writing. Without goals, you just fly by the seat of your pants. Enthusiastic energy is contagious, but without a plan it's not productive. Look at your plan often to motivate your hustle. Below is much of our original plan, written in 2005. We described in detail where we intended to be by the end of 2012 and wrote it as if it had already happened. It doesn't matter what part of your vision statement is realized or if it takes longer than the original time line. What matters is to have a clear vision of where you're going. We recommend using the headers below to guide writing your own visions:

OVERALL VISION: On December 31, 2013, College Hunks Hauling Junk has more than 150 franchise partners located in the fifty largest U.S. cities, with systemwide sales of $50 million.

BRAND VISION: College Hunks Hauling Junk is highly respected and recognized as *the* creative, innovative leader in the junk-removal and labor services industry. Ours is a household name in every major U.S. city. Our brand is more widespread and recognized than that of other companies with similar models. We're the only logical choice for junk removal and labor. Our marketing appeals emotionally to our clients' nostalgic loyalty to the collegiate spirit. Our brand elicits smiles and double takes. No other home service company has exploded on the scene like ours. Our awe-inspiring service keeps clients loyal. Our core value of "Always branding" keeps our company top-of-mind at all times.

CULTURE VISION: College Hunks Hauling Junk is a real-life never-never land *and* fountain of youth combined. The youthful energy and enthusiasm permeating our vibrant company culture help everyone who deals with us feel like a college student on campus. Our team displays youthful vigor. Our values rest squarely on the idea that people, not profits, are our most important asset. There are no employees, just team members. There are no customers, just clients. We don't sell services; we bring clients into our family. Team members are hardworking and full of integrity. The company spirit motivates them to be the best in our league. Clients use our service to share the experience of our fun, youthful company culture. This expedites explosive growth. The business experience gained in every position is something no MBA class provides. Our core value of "Creating a fun, enthusiastic team environment" helps empower team members to meet their professional goals.

LEADERSHIP VISION: This is a company of winners. Our core value is to build leaders. Our slogan "Let Tomorrow's Leaders Haul Your Junk Today" holds true. Everyone is accountable for the vision and improving the brand. We walk, talk, and act like a five-hundred-unit, $100 million operation. *Failure* isn't in our vocabulary. Winning is contagious and fun. Anyone who's not a winner is also not a leader, and therefore isn't on our team. Our core value of "Building leaders" helps empower team members to meet their professional goals.

PROFIT VISION: Our franchisee profits are a top priority. Team members understand what drives profits and make decisions accordingly. They understand the difference between an expense and an investment (see "Expense vs. Investment," page 74). Great care is taken not to confuse them. Our company experiences healthy margins and growing profits each year.

OFFICE VISION: Our Client Loyalty Center (Brand Central) is a vibrant environment. We have thirty-five dedicated sales reps. Clients and franchise partners constantly praise our team members' enthusiasm and personalities. The Tampa headquarters boasts state-of-the-art equipment and has won numerous "Best Workplace" awards.

COMMUNICATION VISION: As in football, our president, GM, offensive and defensive coordinators, coaches, and players have systems in place to make communication efficient and effective. We have huddles at Junk U, morning meetings at the franchise level, weekly meetings with the support team, forum posts, birthday wishes, monthly conference calls, an annual convention, etc., to facilitate improvements and effective operation. Communication between the Client Loyalty Center and the franchisees is seamless, as if they were all in the same office.

CUSTOMER SERVICE VISION: Team member and client loyalty is our top priority. We're not just a junk-removal service. We're a service that makes people happy to know us. We give them relief from their unwanted items and satisfy their labor needs. Clients get an enjoyable experience whenever they interact with us and team members look for ways to create "wow" moments for the client. Happy checks reveal a 99 percent loyalty rating, and answer "yes" to the question of whether they'd use our service again or recommend us. All concerns are addressed and followed up to remedy any issue immediately. We continue to receive awards and recognition for our high customer service standards. Our core value of "Listen, fulfill, and delight" is lived every day to create an unforgettable experience for our clients.

METRICS VISION: Our customized proprietary software has a clear-cut system for tracking key performance indicators, growth, trends, and goals, and compares actual results to projections. Growth is measured on a regular basis, and our company is on track to be a $100 million company by 2015.

IMAGE VISION: Image is everything in this organization. People are buying "College Hunks." Those not in college or not hunks do everything possible to project a clean, crisp, and friendly image. Our youthful energy, charm, and enthusiasm compensate for any lack of looks or age. Team members who don't respect the dress code or image of the brand are let go. The voice clients hear, the trucks they see, and the team members they interact with are clean, friendly, and charming.

MEDIA VISION: College Hunks Hauling Junk is a media phenomenon. We're featured in numerous national and regional media outlets, such as *Fortune Small Business*, *Entrepreneur*, CNN, C-SPAN, *The Daily Show*, *People* magazine, *Good Morning America*, *The Oprah Winfrey Show*, and the *Wall Street Journal*. Our bestselling book has resulted in national tours and increased brand awareness. Our collegiate themes and fun outlook on a blue-collar industry allow us to spread the College Hunks Hauling Junk name like wildfire. Our brand, image, and culture are communicated through hundreds of news articles, television interviews, and Internet blogs. Our primary emphasis is on being a business success first; we leverage the media to help achieve that goal.

SYSTEM VISION: Systems are in place for every aspect of the business, which eliminates guesswork. The Client Loyalty Center is streamlined, with more than thirty reps, two managers, and an infrastructure that measures performance and volume. Our support team has ten field members and two regional managers. Our sales team has a director and two sales reps. Our PR team works around the clock pitching stories to the media. Our systems are the reason people invest in and buy into the College Hunks Hauling Junk brand.

OTHER VISION (JUNK UNIVERSITY): We recently moved into a twenty-thousand-square-foot office overlooking palm trees and pristine fountains in beautiful Tampa. Our Client Loyalty Center, franchise support and training, and marketing department are all here with a common goal of growing and strengthening the brand and the company.

MENTORS VISION: Our board comprises power players, including CEOs of major corporations and other high-profile, successful entrepreneurs. We meet on a quarterly basis to strategize and improve.

SUCCESS VISION: We will never be a success until we recognize that we are already hugely successful. Success as an organization is defined by living our core values, growing profits, and increasing client loyalty.

Start with a vision, create a strategic plan, and live by it.

Share your vision statement with team members. Those that don't get it don't belong on your team. Fill out a goal sheet. We believe that goals are ineffective if they're not written down, about

50 percent effective when they're written digitally, and over 90 percent effective when they're handwritten. We created a long-term vision as well as an initial start-up checklist before launching on a full scale, to ensure that we knew where we were going and how we'd get off the ground. Below is our original start-up checklist. Create your own and take time to make sure you cover everything relevant to your vision. Be as specific as possible. You can visit our Web site at www.effortlessentrepreneur.com and download a free blank goal sheet to create your own.

Task	Notes

1. IDEA
Evaluate Your Idea

2. PLAN

Task	Notes
PART-TIME VS. FULL-TIME (NICK)	Business incubators as start-up option.
BUYING A FRANCHISE INFO	Ask questions. Apply to other companies' franchises. Visit International Franchise Association (www.franchise.org) for more info.
DEFINING YOUR MARKET	Identify your niche. Consider subcontracting opportunities (government, university).
MARKET RESEARCH	Homework tasks such as surveys, competition, primary research, secondary statistics, and focus groups.
NAME ISSUES	Trademark issues, logos, etc.
BUSINESS STRUCTURE	Choosing between LLC, corporation, S corporation, limited partnership, etc. Fill out appropriate PAPERWORK. Consider city and state regulations. Consult lawyer and accountant.

REVISING BUSINESS PLAN	Revise—especially financial statements. Must create monthly projections for three years. Business plan templates at www.effortlessentrepreneur.com
BUSINESS LICENSES AND PERMITS	Investigate zoning and city, county, and state ordinances.
HIRING A LAWYER AND ACCOUNTANT	Shop around; be prepared with business plan and questions. Don't overspend!

3. MONEY

FINANCING WITH FRIENDS AND RELATIVES	Start-up costs worksheets.
HOW TO ACQUIRE INVESTORS	Create a business plan and get feedback from investor groups on feasibility and investment options, angel investors vs. private equity vs. family and friends.
DEBT FINANCING	Loan applications, bank and loan options.
GOVERNMENT LOANS	SBA, minority option?

4. SETTING THE STAGE

CHOOSING A LOCATION	Issues to consider: parking, accessibility, office, shared space, incubators, facility worksheet, leases, lease checklist.
WORKING-FROM-HOME OPTION	Zoning and legality issues. Know when to move.
PROFESSIONAL IMAGE	Visit competitors' sites. Logo—color, graphics, image, business cards, stationery, sign, decals.
INVENTORY	Finding and dealing with suppliers, trade shows, etc.
OFFERING CREDIT TO CUSTOMERS	Accepting credit and debit cards, checks, collecting, merchant status—get referrals.
MAILING AND SHIPPING	Mailing equipment and accounts.

(Continued)

HIRING EMPLOYEES	Consider various positions and alternatives: salary, hourly, part-time, leased, temp.
EMPLOYEE BENEFITS PLAN	Consider various options, follow mandatory laws.
BUSINESS INSURANCE	Cover basics, consider additional options, shop around.

5. GETTING STUFF

EQUIPMENT BASICS	Cover necessities, shop around, consider leasing/buy options.
COMPUTER SYSTEM	Consider necessities, consider additions: printer, scanner, extra computers, etc.
WIRELESS OPTIONS	Consider wireless options—laptops, compatibility of equipment, etc.
PHONES, FAX, COPIERS	Consider options—including Kinko's for starters, 1-800 number, etc.
LEASE OR BUY A CAR	Consider pros and cons of both alternatives. Be sure to test before anything.

6. MARKETING

ADVERTISING	Consider all options—print, media, mail, brochures, etc. Consider costs and benefits. Calculate return on investment.
PROMOTION	Get publicity, targets, releases, network.
HOW TO SELL	This is for contracting business—product, price, placement, promotion. Find similar services' customer base etc. Make appointments, guarantee.
CUSTOMER SERVICE	Set standards and write manual. How to maintain customer loyalty?

7. USING THE INTERNET

USING THE NET FOR SUCCESS	Links for: market research, competition, financing, legal/business forms, taxes, banking, trade associations.
COMPANY WEB SITE	Create a SCRIPT. Shop around for best designer, host, etc.; be able to update it. Find similar "model" sites.
INTERNET FOR ADVERTISING	Search engines, paid searches, affiliates, joint ventures, search engine marketing (SEM), search engine optimization (SEO).

8. BOOKKEEPING

BASICS OF ACCOUNTING	Computer program. Cash or accrual? General ledger, payroll, consult accountant. QuickBooks online.
HOW TO CREATE FINANCIAL STATEMENTS	Understand and be able to create statements and projections.
MANAGING FINANCES	Gross profit margin, breakeven, markup, budget, working capital. Chart of accounts.
WHAT TO KNOW ABOUT TAXES	Consider all issues, consult IRS publications, consult accountant.
FINISHING NOTES	"Success is a reward for hard work." "Setbacks are good teachers." "Failure is not an option."
BUSINESS RESOURCES	Be sure to consult resources listed throughout this book in addition to those listed here.

9. ADDITIONAL SPECIFIC TASKS
FOR COLLEGE HUNKS HAULING JUNK

CELL PHONES	Provide to employees.
TRUCK BOX	Manufacturer?
PAINT, PRINTING, DECALS, LOGOS, ETC.	Signage company?
PARKING	Where to park vehicles.

(Continued)

DUMPING/RECYCLING/DONATING	Where to dispose of and recycle items?
GROWTH PLAN	Direction for growth.
ADDITIONAL IDEAS	
OMAR/NICK JOB DUTIES	Daily and hourly breakdown? Preliminary, during initial operation, after Nick becomes full-time, etc.

EXPENSE VS. INVESTMENT

There's a big difference between an expense and an investment. An investment is money spent with the goal of making a profit or another significant benefit. Buying a fancy car just to drive around in is an expense. We considered all money spent to buy our toll-free phone number and technology to develop our company, purchase our first truck, and develop our brand, goals, vision, and ourselves as investments. We never saw them as expenses, since we had confidence that they'd ultimately give us a significant return by building our company. Spending money to grow your business is an investment in your vision.

Expenses are dollars out of the business that don't produce a return. It's often hard to distinguish between investments and expenses. If our software developers create a bad product, that investment becomes an unnecessary expense. Early expenditures in business are risky, since it's hard to determine what's an investment before it's too late. Decisions are from your gut, without true calculation or evaluation. Our gut said to buy the phone number and that we were ready to franchise and needed to hire industry experts to bring us to the next stage. Almost everything can be rationalized as an investment, but too many expenditures that yield minimal or negative returns can bury a business. Make only the most important investments early on:

- Name and logo
- Web site development with a professional-sounding URL and image
- Vanity phone number if appropriate
- Business card and basic marketing collateral

Shelve others until timing and business warrant them, including software development (off-the-shelf software is more affordable), professional consultants, legal fees that aren't essential, and personal expenses. Investments in your initial brand will evolve. Do your due diligence when making early business investments. Find people in a different industry and ask whom they hired and what they paid, and if they're satisfied with the results. Almost everything is an investment when you start. The challenge is budgeting to determine what you can afford that fits your overall goals.

"BALLIN' ON A BUDGET"

We began with limited resources and means. Many entrepreneurs do. Budget and resource limitations stop some people from pursuing their business dream. But those of us who go forward find ways to compensate. Hands-on smart work, together with careful planning, gets lots of mileage. When we walked into the American Marketing Association marketing awards ceremony in

2006, we felt invisible. Nobody gave us any respect. Advertising firms and bigwigs stayed in their cliques. Everyone was in suits and ties, while we wore our green polos. But we dominated the awards, winning three different categories that evening.

We won the award for Marketing Campaign on a Shoestring Budget, which we named "Ballin' on a Budget." Rappers use this term to create an appearance of wealth when they have limited funds and resources. We certainly stretched dollars to the max. At first Nick thought Omar was crazy when he bought that Range Rover we discussed in chapter 1, but it reinforced our image of being a healthy organization while we were still in our dingy first office. Having a Range Rover got us on a CBS news story and contributed to our signing several large corporate accounts. So we actually got a return on that investment.

You need to keep track of your return on investment (ROI). The ROI is profit minus cost, divided by cost. For example, if you conduct a direct-mail campaign for $1,000 and your company gains $1,500 in profits, then your ROI is $1,500 − $1,000 / $1,000, which equals one-half or 50 percent return on investment. If you gained only $750 in profits, then your ROI is $750 − $1000 / $1000, which is −.25 or MINUS 25 percent ROI. From the start, we created a monthly budget and reviewed it, to know exactly how much money we had on hand. We still do this. On paper you can see exactly what you can afford to spend compared to projected sales. Initially, we shopped for vendors based on price and service. We pitched it as a ground-floor opportunity to work with a company that would grow nationally. We still do business today with those that took a chance and believed in us, and we still beat them up on price whenever possible!

A challenge faced early on was that everything seemed like the next big advertising opportunity or cool marketing tool. Like kids in a candy store, we wanted to do billboards, TV advertising, radio, buses, and more. After extremely expensive mistakes with advertising and shared mailers, we reevaluated what we spent money on to make sure each expenditure would have a true and measurable ROI. We deferred our personal compensation until year two, when we took a small draw, but we reinvested the majority of profits back into the company, since profits drive future growth. To determine the best ways to spend limited funds, evaluate the ROI. Something may seem like a good idea, but if it doesn't directly boost sales, it may not be worth it.

Good financial management is crucial from the beginning. Cash is the oxygen of any business. If you can't manage what comes in and goes out, your business will drown. Plan for that immediately. Get a good accountant who won't overcharge you, take accounting classes, or both. You can't spend haphazardly as you see needs or opportunities. Successful entrepreneurs respect money and understand the need to manage it properly. We quickly jumped into the franchise business and used the best companies and experts to develop our model. We knew it would help our overall cash flow and keep expenses lower in the long run. Decide what works for your budget and try to stick to it.

SYSTEMIZING YOUR BUSINESS

For many people, being an employee seems like the most secure way to earn a living. But it's the most restrictive in terms of building wealth. Being self-employed has tax advantages but you're still reliant on your own production. If our friends who play online poker for a living stop playing, money stops coming in. Business owners create systems that work in their absence. Developing systems is crucial to growing your business.

Create effective systems to keep your business on track and enable individuals to succeed.

As our Fifth Business Commandment explains, your business needs systems for each part of its operations, documented in manuals that employees can use as a guideline for doing their jobs. Systems ensure the quality standards of your business. There should be a script for any phone calls that might be made and for in-person interactions. Everything that an employee would be expected to do in any situation should be spelled out in writing to prevent misunderstandings. If people don't know what should have been done, they didn't study the manual. You want people on your team who do.

The ideal system is bulletproof and covers everything possible. Since perfection can never be achieved, systems must be worked on and updated continually. The best way to avoid business failure is to create the most comprehensive systems you can, allowing for glitches in the system, employee behavior, and the unexpected. Do your best to think of contingency plans for any possible situation you may find yourself in so that if stuff goes wrong, it won't fall on each individual to struggle to adapt.

A good system not only lays out the ideal set of steps for each situation, but also offers protocols for enforcing them. It should also detail what to do if someone or something causes a break in the system. For example, a good system will tell you not only how to hire and train good employees, but how to handle bad or problematic employees who somehow slip through the hiring process. If a system allows for certain budget assumptions, it should ideally also offer ideas for what to do and how to prioritize and cope if those assumptions aren't met.

The reality is that most entrepreneurs, especially early on in the business, get called back into the fire continually as things crop up that the system doesn't cover or the staff doesn't handle properly. The various protocols are the tiers and levels of the system. Just like a machine, the systems have to act in unison on multiple levels and tiers in order to function properly. We thought our D.C. operation was fully systemized when we left it to focus on franchising. However, soon the trucks started breaking down, equipment got lost, and our manager got burned out. At first we were lost and confused. We'd done everything we thought of to create checklists and metrics, and had documented all the standard operating procedures. But without *accountability*, incentives, and enforcement, systems don't get implemented and managed properly.

Guys no longer filled out paperwork properly and trucks weren't maintained regularly, despite the paperwork and truck maintenance logs we'd created. Our first inclination was to blame the manager, but we realized we hadn't put a system in place on the tier above the front-line staff that held the manager accountable for the staff and how they conducted themselves. We needed a system to require the manager to report to us, to define what his responsibilities and accountabilities were, and we needed a protocol for not following the systems. There was one for the front-line employees but not for the management to enforce the front-line systems or for the management systems to be enforced. Businesses require layers of systems that work in unison. Each layer increases the complexity of how the system functions.

Treat your business like an intricate machine. Every part performs a specific and measurable function. Build this machine with the goal of not being part of it down the road. Overseeing it is the role of a true entrepreneur. Sell the machine's products and services to clients and perfect how it operates, but strive to not be the main person operating it. Even if you can't afford a staff yet, identify each position and treat them all as separate responsibilities. Create manuals and training maps for each position so you clearly visualize what's needed, and have them ready when you hire staff. We did every task at first, but treated them all as separate jobs that others would eventually step into.

Begin to develop systems as you analyze each aspect of your business. Detail in a manual what should be covered and why. Spell out the how-tos for each one. Manuals contain all documented information and distribution channels used for training and retraining. Eventually this information can be disseminated by more effective methods, such as on the Internet or in training videos. Create checklists for each position's daily tasks. Just as an airplane pilot goes down his checklist, each team member in your company should use one. Positions are never locked in place, since the organization continues to evolve. But it's crucial to define them from the beginning.

Work ON the business from the outside, not IN it.

Our first step for developing systems was creating a position chart describing each position in the company. Next we detailed what each position was responsible for and wrote manuals, scripts, accountabilities, metrics, and checklists for each one, even specifying how staff should dress, speak, and answer the phone. Systems ALWAYS evolve, but our outline below illustrates how systems work for our business. Use it as a guideline to create your own.

- **People systems.** What they wear; what they say; how to interact with clients; how to maintain a loyal client base.
- **Marketing and sales systems.** How to position your product or service and how to generate those leads and close them.
- **Leadership systems.** Meeting rhythms, vision, brand, and values; how will you or your leadership team lead the troops? How often will you meet? What will you measure and discuss in each meeting? What are the overall core values, brand philosophy, and long-term vision?
- **Financial management and administration systems.** How will you keep your books, and review your profit-and-loss and financial statements each month? What are your key metrics and key performance indicators that dictate the health of your financial conditions as a business?
- **Client loyalty/customer service systems.** What are your service standards? What are your above and beyond services? What is your service recovery protocol when something goes bad? How do you foster loyal clients?

- **Operational systems.** What happens day to day? What is the daily checklist for the operational staff?
- **HR systems.** Whom will you hire? How will you hire? How will you train staff?
- **Software.** What software will you use to help automate processes and keep them streamlined to increase efficiency?

As a business owner, make yourself replaceable. Ask, "How would this business function without me?" Write down in detail five ways that your daily operations could be systemized better and HOW you created and improved your systems. *If I had to franchise my business (or position) I'd have to systemize _____.* Keep in mind that even if you systemize your business to the extent that you can remove yourself from the day-to-day operations, ultimately, you still must be the leader. Steve Jobs and Michael Dell are examples of company founders who built perfectly systemized and gigantic megacompanies, then had to return to resurrect the companies when sales dropped or new competitors threatened their marketplace position.

Finding a balance between working IN and working ON the business during a company's infancy is tricky, which is why many businesses fail in the first year. We recognized that anyone could sling junk and that our being on the trucks didn't add value. Then our priorities changed from working IN the business to generate *income* to working ON developing systems for the business to create *growth*.

IMPLEMENTING LESSONS FROM MISTAKES

When entrepreneurs fail, it's usually because they didn't learn from their mistakes. After doing something once, they failed again by repeating what didn't work the first time. It's important to recognize this and approach mistakes with caution. If you make a mistake, be cognizant of the error, analyze it to see what went wrong, figure out how you could have done it more successfully, and make a conscious effort to avoid repeating it.

Mistakes are problems only if you do not learn from them.

For example, we forgot to get maintenance on time for our truck when we started out—an extremely costly mistake. But we didn't learn. Sure enough, problems happened again, since we didn't keep proper track of maintenance. Had we not learned at that point, we could have hurt our company by taking years off our truck's life. Fortunately, that second unnecessary expense woke us up to putting a system in place for maintenance. Our vision included a fleet of trucks, so we needed to keep them in good shape. Just as we recharge electronic devices so they don't go dead, we must do upkeep on tools for running the business and be vigilant after a mistake to make sure to do it better next time.

Create a journal that documents every issue that comes up. Take it a step further by having separate headers, such as "Customer Complaints," "Employee Issues," and "Software Problems." Every time something happens, document it under the corresponding header and answer these questions:

- Why did it happen?
- What precautions can be taken to prevent it from happening again?
- How can improvement on this issue be measured?
- Are there issues that are similar to this one that could arise?
- How can those similar issues be prevented?

Mistakes allow you to develop and adopt better systems. For example, we foolishly spent hundreds of thousands of dollars on marketing campaigns that got no results. Had we continued the same campaigns with the same people and wasted more money, they'd have been useless mistakes. Instead, we learned what not to do. Trying different strategies and failing at some allows you to identify what marketing methods do work. Waiting too long to learn from mistakes causes many businesses to fail.

There's a difference between making a mistake and being irresponsible. Mistakes are carefully thought-out decisions that end up being incorrect. Making reckless decisions or ignoring common sense is inexcusable. Carelessness or critical mistakes can send a business into bankruptcy. Don't suffer from the Superman syndrome and jump off a cliff, expecting not to crash. Every day the headlines are full of major companies like Enron, World-Com, and Lehman Brothers whose leaders' irresponsible decisions brought down the dreams and livelihoods of many people.

The clichéd definition of insanity is doing the same thing over and over, and expecting a different result. If something doesn't work the first time, try something different. Don't expect different results if you don't change your approach or technique. When you can't get past Level 1 on a video game but continue the same strategy, you'll get bored and eventually stop playing. Embrace mistakes and react accordingly or they'll become habits—bad ones—and WILL occur again and again. If you search for a viable solution, you'll find one. Mistakes teach if you let them!

DOING THE HUSTLE

Once you recognize and harness your entrepreneurial vision and energy, it's time to hustle and grow. The more you hustle and the more passionate you are about achieving goals, the greater your chance for growth. Our vision was clear when we started. Even before making a profit, we didn't blink twice at spending $13,000 to buy our 1-800-Junk-USA phone number or hesitate to hire an attorney to trademark our name and brand. We weren't afraid to spend every penny, including developing state-of-the-art software to run our business and scale it out nationally. You have to make significant decisions, including:

- *People decisions:* How can you increase satisfaction among staff and clients?
- *Strategy decisions:* How can you grow sales?
- *Execution decisions:* How can you improve profits and efficiency?
- *Cash decisions:* How can you best control your bank account?

Develop staff, client, and community loyalty.

Your client base is the overall health of your business. The more harmonious your relationships, the healthier your business and the more it grows and flourishes. Create a system for customers to evaluate the service. We measure the level of satisfaction by assessing client "net promoter score" (NPS). We survey clients after every job to assess their likelihood of using our service again and referring us to others. If clients rate us 9–10, they're promoters; 7–8 is a neutral rating; and 1–6 makes them detractors. Average the total scores and that's our net promoter score.

"Thank you" can't be expressed enough. We instruct team members to use it often. Personally thank clients, investors, vendors, and team members. Handwritten and personal notes work best. Text messages or e-mails do not count. When you do your best to maintain goodwill with all the people you work with or sell to, you've created the best environment in which to hustle and grow your business.

CHAPTER 5

TILL DEATH DO US PART
Creating Partnerships Without Fists

There's a Saturday-morning cartoon called *Pinky and the Brain*. The title characters are genetically engineered mice living at Acme Labs. The Brain is a genius, while Pinky is somewhat feebleminded. They initiate creative and hilarious schemes for world domination that ultimately fail. However, with great persistence, they continue working to "try to take over the world!" Their shared vision makes them a solid team. While Nick is no genius and Omar isn't feebleminded, we relate to *Pinky and the Brain*. It illustrates that when partners agree on the values, vision, and culture of their business, they can come together despite differences. Just as one day these mice may take over their little world, we plan to take over the world of junk removal—together!

WORKING TOGETHER

"We should start a business!"

"Yeah, that would be awesome!"

We frequently had that kind of exchange during high school. Often friends dream over a beer about starting a business. What better way to embark on a high-risk, high-return venture than with a close friend? After all, you can share the burden of losses and enjoy the triumphs together. Choosing to work with a partner is more appealing to people who prefer team sports to individual ones. As a basketball player, Nick relied on his teammates. Winning each game was based on operating in perfect unison. When each teammate contributes his strengths, the team wins. When egos rule, teams implode.

Most entrepreneurs face a partnership dilemma. Some prefer to go it alone. Others feel more comfortable sharing a stake in the business and its problems. You may start solo, realize there are too many balls to juggle, and seek out a partner, who is more likely to be committed to the business than an employee would be. That can make giving up a piece of the business worth it. Each partnership opportunity should be weighed carefully before jumping in. Decide if what you give up is worth the gain.

There are always people smarter than you—hire them!

The obvious advantage of being sole owner is that you reap 100 percent of the rewards. Like athletes playing an individual sport, you're accountable for every shot you take and own everything you do. Problems or failures are your responsibility. You don't get all the credit for success, but you get blamed for all failures. Just as it can be scary for a golfer on the eighteenth green who needs to sink a putt to win, it can be scary for a business owner with 100 percent equity making all the critical decisions. If you start solo, it's CRUCIAL to hire the right people to complement your strengths and weaknesses. Find people smarter than you, who might treat the business as if it were their own. Business is a team sport. You must develop a team, with a partner or not.

We've always played team sports. The idea of having a teammate to share victories and give support is appealing to us. The old cliché "There's no *i* in *team*" is part of our protocol. A true leader shares credit with the team for his accomplishments. A partner can seem like a crutch but is beneficial if leveraged effectively. If the division of labor and effort are shared equitably, much more can be accomplished than one individual could achieve alone.

If you want a partner, choose carefully. When we were on the reality TV show *Shark Tank* to pitch our sister concept—College Foxes Packing Boxes—to a panel of investors for financial consideration, the sharks weren't interested, since it wasn't operational yet. But they offered money for a percentage of College Hunks Hauling Junk and tried to entice us into giving up a portion of our baby. We declined. Their input and expertise could have accelerated our growth. But the terms weren't worth the percentage they wanted. We felt confident about reaching our goals without them.

The opportunity to share successes and failures with a best friend is the best part of our achievements. Having one as a business partner makes victories sweeter. We've gone through ups and downs together. The experience stirs excitement and a sense of possibility like those that childhood friends create when beating a video game together or winning the peewee football championship.

When something goes wrong, Nick calls Omar to vent and get ideas for handling it. He can call friends from outside the business, but Omar has a vested interest in whatever Nick complains about. We support each other well. When one of us is stuck for an answer, the other often finds it. For example, Nick met someone from USAirways who asked if College Hunks Hauling Junk could clear out an entire warehouse at Reagan National Airport. Nick said, "Yes," with no idea how we'd actually get it done. But you NEVER turn down opportunities to make money at the beginning.

Nick was scared and immediately called Omar: "We might get a HUGE job from USAirways but I don't think we can do it." Omar shouted, "Are you crazy? We'll figure it out!" We crunched numbers, hired guys to help, and found a way. Our plan improved efficiency enough to get the job done by the one-week deadline for the client. We did the job for a lower price than we usually charge and still made money! A partner to brainstorm with is like a study buddy in school to do homework with and copy answers from. Inevitably, you figure out the answers to problems. In a partnership you're allowed to share answers.

One day Nick said, "Dude, we'll go out of business if we don't pay more attention to how we spend money." Omar was surprised but confident it would be fine. Nick lost sleep trying to figure out where the money was going. He was beyond stressed. Having someone calm and sure they'd make it work validated his choice of business partner.

A business partnership isn't that different from a marriage. You find the right person and hope to nurture a good relationship. You both must be there for the long haul and prepared for tough times. On our very first day, we lifted couches in pouring rain and mud and looked at each other, thinking, Are we really quitting good jobs to do this? Yes! We were in it together, friends and business partners, for better or worse, like marriage.

SEEKING PARTNERS WITH PARALLEL VALUES, VISION, AND CULTURE

Successful businesses have a winning team mentality with a shared common goal and accountability for each person's role, just as each member of a football team has a specific position. A quarterback may get more attention than linebackers but couldn't do his job without linemen blocking for him. Businesses that struggle most are those with prima donnas or people with personal agendas that don't match the company's overall vision.

When formulating a partnership, the biggest considerations are your strengths and weaknesses, individual visions, and division of labor. Omar is our visionary and sets the bar high. When he sets a goal for something huge, Nick usually says, "You're crazy. Okay, let's figure out how we'll do it." And we do. Omar paints the picture and tells the story, Nick challenges him, and then we work together to make it happen. Nick is more oriented to Xs and Os and obsessive-compulsive. Omar is more charismatic, personable, and visionary. When one of us sees the other veer from his role, he pushes him to step up and take care of business.

Age and marital status should be considered when selecting a business partner. These factors could affect each other's vision. If one of us got married and had kids tomorrow, his role, responsibilities, and priorities would shift and have a profound effect on the business, potentially causing resentment if work effort and productivity dropped. It's imperative to address these issues in your partnership agreement. Misaligned goals and values can bury a partnership, whether they start misaligned or slip over time.

Start with a vision, create a strategic plan, and live by it.

Three primary factors hold a partnership together: values, vision, and culture. The partnership succeeds only if those factors remain aligned. Otherwise, any disruption or hiccup in the business can topple it. We often get to the brink of physical confrontation, but after our hissy fits we get back to business and continue working toward our common vision. Each partner should write a vision statement prior to entering a partnership and then review the other's to look for similarities and discrepancies. If there are many discrepancies in the vision, chances are the partnership won't work. If they're similar, use them both to forge the company vision. Rewrite it each year to confirm that you're still aligned.

Each of us wrote his individual vision at the beginning of our business, and our visions were frighteningly similar. We merged the two individual visions to create our company vision, which we discussed in chapter 4. You and your prospective partner should write your visions according to the outline in that chapter and review them before committing to the partnership. Do this at least once a year to assess the partnership's health. If your visions are out of sync, so is your ability to build a solid business together.

Trust is a huge factor between partners. If you don't completely trust the person you're thinking of sharing a business with, you'll have trouble down the road. Suspicions can come up.

Accusations cause feuding and can lead to one trying to rip off the other. Make sure you ask enough questions before you take any steps forward with a potential partner. If you have any doubts at all, wait until you can work them out.

People often rush into partnerships out of convenience or to have someone to share the risk with, but the consequences can be devastating if the partners' visions and values are misaligned. A two-headed monster can emerge even years after you begin. Breakups are very costly and can kill a business. Arguing against partnerships, however, is like arguing against getting married. Marriage has indescribable tangible and intangible benefits. It's the same with business partnerships. More than 50 percent of marriages are said to end in divorce, which can be ugly and expensive. Yet people still get married. Business partnerships are no different. The key is making sure you choose the right partner and are 100 percent confident that your visions and values are in alignment to prevent divorce.

DIFFICULTIES

Working with a friend can backfire. A business is often a train wreck, tornado, and earthquake all in one. Time flashes by, stuff goes wrong almost daily, and things break down and get lost, especially when systems aren't in place yet. Stress can cause you to panic and strain the partner relationship. Communication and reactions to strains make or break a partnership. It's easier for one friend to "free-ride" off another. Resentment builds in whoever does the bulk of the work and sets you up for failure.

Work ON the business from the outside, not IN it.

Someone we know started a business with his best friend. Jordan was the creative and visionary. Bob did sales and handled numbers. Their operation grew to over $1 million in annual sales. Bob was satisfied but the visionary Jordan saw it growing to over $10 million. When sales dropped, Jordan didn't want to blame Bob, since they were best friends and built the business together. The partnership was a fifty-fifty deal, which was dangerous because no one person had final control. Their visions were different. Bob had an employee, small-business mentality. He was content working IN the business, not ON it. Jordan wanted his business to grow.

After several tense months, Jordan knew he had to split to pursue his vision. He hired attorneys to buy out control of his company so he could grow it to the level he envisioned. It was ugly. Like a married couple without a prenup, they had no exit plan. Bob was after blood, while Jordan felt ripped off. He paid through the nose to end the relationship. They lost a true friendship, and the business suffered extensively too. Detecting partnership problems early is critical. You must decide to work things out, or cut ties and salvage the friendship, if possible. Business partners should prepare by spelling everything out in a partnership agreement.

PARTNERSHIP AGREEMENTS

Much like a prenuptial agreement, a partnership agreement is essential before embarking on this relationship. It should outline all protocols and what-ifs. What happens if one partner dies, or decides to stop working, or has a drug problem, or if there is an irreconcilable disagreement? All what-ifs should be spelled out in the agreement, yet people still foolishly embark on partnerships without one.

Details of the partnership should be addressed up front to avoid confrontation down the road, including buy/sell agreements, operating agreements, and the structure of compensation. For example, when Omar bought a new computer for $1,800, Nick already had one that had been purchased before starting the business. Omar's compensation decreased that month by the cost of the computer. It was most important to put our expected commitment to the business on paper. While it had been discussed verbally, we committed in writing to devote at least thirty-five hours a week to the business. We also addressed the protocol for outside business ventures that could affect our primary business. We didn't want conflicts of interest or bad feelings later.

Create effective systems to keep your business on track and enable individuals to succeed.

The biggest danger is unspoken and/or unclear expectations. Your agreement should define the friendship and relationship following a split. It can be tough to keep your personal life and business separate, even with an agreement. There should also be a system in place for confronting each other if one partner's performance slacks.

It's important to have a good lawyer as an unbiased adviser for putting together the agreement, and to keep the partnership agreement on file and ensure that it's enforced should an issue arise. Lawyers can make recommendations from observing other failed and successful partnerships. Each partner should have another lawyer review the agreement to make sure his or her individual interests are protected. Go to www.effortlessentrepreneur. com for samples of clauses in partnership agreements and other resources and updates.

WORKING WELL TOGETHER

Working together for the good of your company takes a conscious effort. Omar pictures the grand scheme and sees it materializing, but his patience and ability to grasp numbers or fine details are weaker. Nick shares his vision and brings an important skill set—financial and economic understanding and operational organization.

Many friendships and marriages fail over business disagreements, hence the saying "Don't mix business with pleasure." Our comfort level as friends permits us to talk straight and keep resentment from being buried. When resentment is stifled, it surfaces in negative and destructive ways. We have a unique method of handling frustrations—squabbling and fighting, almost like two kids on a playground. We get into heated arguments, cuss each other out, and even come close to fisticuffs. But at the end of the day the business always takes priority. Our visions and values are so well aligned that no squabble will undermine that. And even if we haven't always been completely mature about everything (just ask our team members who've had to listen to us), by venting our anger we at least make sure it isn't harbored until the business relationship is beyond repair. As our partnership has evolved, we've learned to behave more maturely around others, and to look for better ways to vent our frustrations or disagreements. But we still always try to say what's on our mind.

When we're out on the town business usually comes up, but it's no longer work to us. It's more like basketball teammates, discussing a practice or strategies for the next game. Respect for each other keeps us tight. It's important to respect each other's strengths and weaknesses. If you can't respect your teammate, you can't win the game. Shaquille O'Neal and Kobe Bryant didn't like each other but respected each other and won three championships together. Once they stopped respecting each other, the team fell apart.

When we started College Hunks Hauling Junk, Omar wanted a majority ownership, since he wrote the original business plan, but Nick wasn't comfortable moving forward without a fifty-fifty split, which we ultimately agreed to. This is contrary to most business advice because if it's an even split, no one is ultimately accountable. But we were clear about everything in our agreement.

OVERCOMING DISAGREEMENTS

Disagreements arise from myriad issues—relations with employees, marketing, sales, and many others. Remember what's most important for the good of your company. The biggest partnership breaker is money. We know how much we take and what we put back in. We're in this for the long haul, not to make a quick buck. Our personal pride and sweat equity are invested. It's in our best interests to see the venture through. We've disagreed on how much to spend on marketing. Nick pulled the trigger on a plan that cost $15,000 when cash was tight. Omar was unhappy, since he hadn't been consulted. Your partnership agreement must outline what level of expenditure requires both partners' votes to proceed.

We sometimes fight about working styles. Nick gets frustrated with Omar's carelessness and his cavalier, "things will fall into place" mentality. Omar gets frustrated with Nick's "play by the book," punch-in and punch-out approach. We get mad at each other when things go wrong. If we weren't best friends, this might cause a serious disruption in the business, or even kill it. But we always put our gripes aside and get back to work.

Minor issues can snowball into larger problems. The smallest hitch in our daily operation, like a flat tire or an upset customer, can cause stress that sends us into an uproar. In retrospect, most fights are petty bickering. After many arguments we learned not to sweat the small stuff, and in reality, everything is small compared to the big picture. Communication can be awkward during a disagreement, especially if a relationship isn't as comfortable as a close friendship. No matter how angry we get with each other, we express it however we see fit and move on. We don't want disagreements to unravel our business. That's good motivation to get things out and resolve issues that would otherwise cause resentment.

If you get angry and stop communicating, your partnership won't work and your business won't succeed. It can be hard to solve problems by shouting or arguing, so if possible cool off before you discuss problems. Try to respect each other's views and listen carefully with an open mind. When Omar had a gut feeling that a prospective franchisee wouldn't be a good fit, Nick considered only the dollar signs from the sale. But Omar spoke persuasively enough to sway Nick. If one partner feels particularly strong about a situation or issue, she should speak up and make the other listen.

SHOULD YOU TAKE ON A PARTNER?

When you consider taking on a partner, ask yourself, "Can I do it on my own?" Have a clear picture of where you want to take your business, how you'll get there, and how quickly you need to arrive. If you can realize that picture by simply hiring people to help, it may be okay to ride solo. However, you need to consider all aspects of doing it alone, including the pitfalls of having only employees with no vested interest in the company's success.

Ask yourself, "Even if I can do it myself, do I want to?" There's both an emotional and a practical aspect to consider, and they often aren't aligned. The emotional one requires you to look inside to determine what's really important. Even if you achieve greatness by yourself, would you like to share the triumphs with a teammate who has a similar vested interest? Emotionally you may choose a friend or relative, since it feels comfortable. But if that person's values, vision, and culture aren't aligned with yours from a businesses perspective, any adversity could cause a huge rift, both business and personal.

On the practical side, even if you can do it on your own, would you prefer not having to do 100 percent of the work? Some people don't mind sharing a portion of the company to keep from doing it all. The question then becomes, "How much do I share and how do I know what this person will contribute?" When you identify your strengths, weaknesses, and unique abilities, try to partner with someone who can balance your weaknesses and share the load evenly. Before you agree to work with a partner, ask yourself these questions and think hard about your answers:

- Can I share the spotlight or be under a microscope?
- Am I willing to share the decision-making power?
- Am I able to lead by myself?
- Am I willing to respect the boundaries and needs of someone with ownership in the company?
- Am I willing to take a minority stake in the company or do I need a majority?
- What are my strengths? What do I not like to do?
- What are my ultimate goals for this business?
- Am I able to bear the entire weight of the business on my shoulders?

Any venture you embark on involves risk from unknown variables that come with a new business. Adding a partner increases those unknown risks. A person can get lazy and not uphold his end. Neither of you is wholly accountable for what could go wrong, so partnering creates a false sense of security that you don't have when you start solo. If you and your partner don't work as hard as possible together to launch the business, it can fizzle and die. Unless who is accountable for what is spelled out in your partnership agreement, there's no one captain to steer the ship of the business. Fingers pointed at each other do no good. You and your partner must both be fully committed and ready to do whatever it takes to succeed.

Don't jump into bed with the first person who gets excited about your business plan or who has cash to invest. Spend time together to assess the kind of personality you'd be working with. Does anything annoy you now? If so, it will only get worse under pressure. Make sure it's someone who can be a team player and complement what you bring to the company. Check references. Ask why this person wants to be your partner. The wrong partner can sink your dream fast. The right one can create a harmonious team like ours, making the game much more enjoyable, rewarding, and productive.

CHAPTER 6

PLAYING THE GAME
A New Spin on a Traditional Idea

During college, Nick returned from class, loaded up Play-Station2, and tackled *Grand Theft Auto II: Vice City*. He was obsessed with it, playing it in the morning, going to class, then returning to play more before passing out, exhausted. The game was captivating. It cast the gamer in the role of an ex-con named Tommy working to conquer the corrupt Vice City. Playing it allowed Nick to immerse himself in a world and a story that were every bit as exciting, tense, and dramatic as his favorite gangster movies.

Nick would phone Omar, who was playing the same game, for strategies and ideas to reach the next level or defeat the next bad guy. Video games take on a life of their own, and kids who play them become engulfed in the imaginings and excitement this virtual world creates. It's like you're teleported into your favorite movie. As technology and entertainment evolve, the lines between what's real and what's fantasy become more and more blurred, as evidenced by the world's obsession with reality TV, and now the virtual worlds created on the Internet with REAL money being spent, which further blurs lines. Baskin-Robbins actually sells franchises in the online virtual world known as Second Life.

We loved playing video games and escaping into this virtual world. But the day-to-day challenges of running and growing College Hunks Hauling Junk provide the same rush we felt playing games. We delayed gratification and hedonistic opportunities to build the business. It's been worth it to get to higher and higher levels of success in branding our company, adding franchises, and increasing our revenues—like getting to more challenging levels of a game. The desire to put points on the board and win is an innate characteristic in many of us. Harnessing that desire when building a business leads to successful entrepreneurship.

THE GAME OF BUILDING A BUSINESS

If you sit an average person in front of anything halfway intriguing and explain that it keeps score and has rankings with rewards, he'll become obsessed. Hence the popularity of video games, sports, and dating. Harnessing those tendencies to view building a business as playing a game leads to more fun pursuing success. Many of the plots and challenges in games resemble situations in business. You must be adventurous, on your toes, and ready to jump on problems or opportunities the moment they arise.

For example, the plot of the PlayStation game *Metal Gear Solid* gets you thinking in action terms. It's considered a classic by many players, but not because it has fights or challenges you can't find elsewhere. In fact, it's full of elements found in many games, like soldiers with guns, ninjas, and robots. What makes

Metal Gear Solid popular is the story it builds around those elements, so that those soldiers and ninjas have fascinating backstories, full of twists and turns. Each enemy is a fully developed character, and every fight or challenge you face plays an important role in the story. People think of video games as mindless entertainment, but in fact, the games we loved most made us think and care about the characters and story. It's the same thing in business. Entrepreneurs and employees work harder and like it more if they're challenged and excited, if they care about what they do, and if they are given opportunities to think and advance their own personal story.

Metal Gear's story line of epic battles and emotional intrigue, makes you do more than play the game. It makes you *love* and remember it forever. Now running our company provides the same fulfillment. In fact, once we started it, we never touched a video game controller again. The adrenaline rush from playing a virtual game was no longer there. It's in our business!

We felt something more exciting, more of a rush, more real than a game. Launching our own business made us feel like we'd been teleported into our own real-life Vice City or *Metal Gear Solid*. We didn't deal with mob bosses or nuclear-armed tanks, but scored points by making money, completing missions, and reaching business milestones. Adding clients, expanding press coverage, boosting revenue, and selling franchises increased our score and took us to higher levels in the "game" of business. Like playing video games, we encountered obstacles (flat tires, upset clients), tackled challenges (making payroll, juggling multiple jobs), navigated past competition, dealt with regulators, and worked toward reaching the next level (purchasing more trucks, adding new locations).

Most important, like playing video games, we're in control of our own destiny. But while games have a reset button, in business you keep on going. We know if we reach "Game Over" with College Hunks Hauling Junk we'll be forced to start from scratch, start a different business, or get a job. That motivates us to keep playing. Instead of PlayStation, we play the game of building a junk-removal empire, which is ultimately more satisfying than any video game, since we're able to enjoy the tangible real-life benefits and rewards of winning that a video game can't provide, like vacations, a boat, and celebrations with our team and franchisees! A million points in a game is nice, but a million bucks in real life is a whole lot better.

PLAYING FOR HIGHER LEVELS

Each level of our business game gets more complex and difficult. Level 1 is the simplest, with few surprises, so you get used to the controls and feel safe. Some people are content staying there forever, knowing that if they move up a level it gets more difficult. Some want to move up and try to beat the game. Decide how far to play and when to put down the controller. While some visions seem ambitious, they may not be as ambitious as those of Apple Computer CEO Steve Jobs. He needs a lot to beat his score and hasn't stopped playing the game yet!

We look at our business in terms of levels because it helps keep us motivated and also helps us budget and plan. Video games have levels for a reason. They keep players motivated and organized. Players know what's needed to reach a certain level before they can unlock certain items or benefits. As you build your business, thinking in terms of reaching levels provides clear-cut, short-term goals that will seem attainable and can motivate you and your staff, even when the long-term visions (or endgame goals) are still far off. Work becomes more fun when you know what you're working for and you know the reward when you reach the goal.

In many role-playing games, not only do you gradually gain new items as you play, but when your character reaches a higher level, he gains a lot of cool stuff, like greater powers and more health at that specific moment. Reaching levels means reaching a series of milestones, with each offering an immediate reward when you hit it. In business, the rewards for reaching your milestones may be more money, greater recognition by your peers, increased business, company expansion, and whatever else you earn from your efforts. Each milestone can set you up to reach for the next one. Plan ahead for what your reward might be to motivate yourself to work hard to reach your short-term goals, knowing that they're stepping-stones to the long-term ones.

If you just jump behind the controls of your business without trying to reach certain milestones (levels), you'll probably fail due to boredom or lack of goal setting. Video games, sports, and business all follow the same principles. The more time you spend playing with purpose, the better you get. The better you get, the higher your score will be.

Start with a vision, create a strategic plan, and live by it.

Our business started as a Level 1 when we took Omar's mom's van, hauled junk ourselves, and collected the money. We took it to the next level by deciding to brand our business, get a real truck, create marketing materials, do it full-time, and hire employees. Level 2 was exponentially harder and more complex than Level 1. We had to train our staff, monitor their actions, and pay salaries. When you go up levels in a video game, you're given special powers, weapons, or items you didn't have before. It's the same in business. The powers won't be a supergun to kill enemies. They may be money, contacts, clients, systems, equipment, or infrastructure.

Each business defines its own levels, just as some games are easier than others. It's up to you to set your goals and what happens when you reach them. Unlike games, you set the rules for your business. We're quite a few levels up now, with many franchise partners across the country. Our complexity level increased dramatically with an increased staff and more locations. To our advantage, we have huge client and media contact lists, vendors who bend over backward for us, cash for advertising and development, the expertise of advisers and executives, and technology that ties it together. So we've worked level by level to continue to up our game score. Our goal is to own everything. We own our brand, systems, and business model.

Create effective systems to keep your business on track and enable individuals to succeed.

Sometimes prospective franchise buyers ask, "Why do I need you? I can start my own junk-hauling company." It's hard not to chuckle. A Level 1 or 2 business going up against a much higher-level one is like Bambi throwing down with Godzilla. If we offer a special promotion, e-mails go to twenty thousand loyal followers. We have executives who spend their entire day selling nationwide to corporate clients. Our Web site is found on the first page of Google for our key search terms. McDonald's doesn't care if a burger restaurant opens nearby. We're not nearly at that level, but we are established with systems and branding in place, so our franchises also begin at an elevated level of business instead of struggling to start up from Level 1.

Business success doesn't hinge on what your business is. If you're willing to advance to higher levels, ANY business can become successful. The same system of *vision, branding, innovation, PR, passion,* and *drive* that got College Hunks Hauling Junk to its level can be implemented to start anything from a Web business, to a restaurant chain, to a vacuum shop, to any other kind of business, and grow it just as quickly. Skill does play a role in the game. There's obviously a difference in skill level between a local coffee shop owner and Howard Schultz, whose vision built Starbucks. But the beauty of entrepreneurship is that you can be at the lowest level and still make a decent living. And even at Level 1, you're still farther along than everyone still stuck slaving away in the corporate rat race. You can't win the game if you don't play.

Just as a basketball player takes thousands of shots to improve his game and a gamer plays over and over to reach higher levels, entrepreneurs must hone their craft and skill. NBA players may be born with certain gifts but still work tirelessly to be the best. The same is true with entrepreneurs. Train yourself with discipline, desire, and passion to be the best. Even if you're talented or find early success, don't stop learning. LeBron James was a hoops prodigy and yet continues to be the first to arrive to warm up before a game and the last to leave practice. To reach higher levels, be committed to improving your ability to build your business.

THE GAME OF INTERNAL COMPETITIONS

We initiated a lot of internal competition in our company. Our staff members get moving when we challenge them to surpass one another's efforts, as many of them do playing video games. We instituted sales competitions and vote competitions (to see which employees could get the most testimonials from clients and votes for Hunk of the Month), which was just another way to generate loyalty and a loyal client database. We also created competition among the different locations across the country.

Competition between franchises began when teams from Virginia challenged those from Maryland to a "Haul-Off" after separate branches opened. They played pranks on each other to liven up the competition. The Virginia teams issued a challenge to see which branch could haul more junk. The challenge was accepted, to last for six months. Instead of trying to extinguish the rivalry, we fueled it by offering winners a three-night trip to the Bahamas, if they followed the rules and regulations. There was an article on the newswire describing a rivalry erupting between our Maryland and Virginia branches. It included our Web site and info about the company, so it was good PR. As College Hunks Hauling Junk grew, so did our ideas for creating competition.

Just as a coach reviews his team's stats after a big game, we began posting monthly "Box Scores" with sales numbers for each location, average job size, and total jobs completed, and we ranked all the locations against one another. Each location could see its place in the competition at any time. The game was on! This not only motivated each location director; it also motivated team members of each location to push and try to put up bigger numbers. All our franchisees wanted to up their game. No longer were we worried about the outside competition or competing for market share. Instead, we pushed one another to improve.

Small, friendly rivalries began to emerge. Our L.A. operation began talking trash to our Orlando operation and vice versa. Each was around $250K in sales and wanted to beat the other one to $300K. This motivated them to get to that level faster. We instituted special awards at our annual convention (which we called our "college reunion") and gave awards for Top Sales, Highest Average Job Size, Best Client Loyalty Rating (we measured client loyalty not satisfaction), and Franchisee of the Year. Each winner received a plaque and a special gift. Surprisingly, peer recognition was the most coveted reward.

We instituted the same kind of award structure on the team-member level as well for things like Highest Sales, Average Job Size, and Best Client Loyalty Rating. Team members lead the morning dispatch huddles to help them recognize and understand the numbers. By measuring and rewarding facets of your business that most influence growth and encouraging competition, you can generate a much more energizing buy-in from team members. It makes work fun and interesting. When managed properly, internal competition is an extremely powerful tool. Challenges make most people want to get to the next level of their game, which improves our business.

If you just tell team members what the goals are without tying them to a tangible reward and/or competition, it won't generate the same results. It's also extremely helpful to hire people who seem to thrive on competition. They're more likely to be motivated by it. Your team should have winners and leaders. If they can't rally behind some friendly competition, they don't belong on the team. As long as egos don't interfere and everyone recognizes that it's all part of the greater goal—to beat the real competition—it's very effective. It's difficult to measure how well you are doing against outside competition, but you can always compare your current and previous performances as well as how others within your organization or different departments compare, since, as the saying goes, "What gets measured gets managed."

Creating competitions within the company is difficult when you have only one or two employees as a start-up. How can you choose Employee of the Month? That was our difficulty too. We couldn't create those types of things until there were enough employees to make it work. But it can still be useful to put competitions on the board from day one: record sales days, most customer compliments, and other statistics can span a team member's past, present, and future.

SCORE! REACHING THE MILLION-DOLLAR MILESTONE

In the beginning, a million dollars in annual sales seemed farfetched, but we really chased it aggressively because we ardently wanted to belong to the Entrepreneurs' Organization, a member organization for business owners of companies with annual sales over $1 million. How good it feels to say we hit $1 million in sales in our second year! When we attended the Entrepreneurs' Organization's twentieth-anniversary event in Las Vegas, we were blown away by the energy and dynamic personalities in attendance.

Reaching this level was far better than attaining a new video game level. It was the first time we'd been around people so energetic, passionate, and entrepreneurial. We felt like we'd found an island of people just like us—not executives or wealthy investors but people who built businesses from scratch, including a guy from Hong Kong who manufactures toy Nerf guns. Being around people with this knack for entrepreneurship, vision, and business was inspiring. We were in the special club of million-dollar companies—the youngest members by far. We got to hear Steve Wynn speak, watch a private concert by KISS, and then took a private side trip to the Playboy Mansion in L.A. as part of the organization.

People laughed in the beginning when we declared that we'd far surpass $1 million in annual sales. We knew we'd laugh later. The only one who must believe in your idea is YOU—enough to know that you can take your business up the levels to success that seems impossible to everyone else. If we'd bought into doubts, we'd still be playing video games, trying to beat the corporate system. Do your research, make a plan, find your unique angle, and market like crazy. Naysayers can stop you or fuel your determination to succeed. We used them as fuel. Now that we've far surpassed the million-dollar level, naysayers still try to understand how two young guys who loved to party built a multimillion-dollar empire out of junk.

CHAPTER 7

PEOPLE EQUITY
Building Staff and Client Loyalty

When Nick was five, his older sister made frozen lemonade in a big pitcher and opened up shop on their front stoop. She made a sign advertising "Lemonade—25 cents." But Nick assumed they'd charge $1 per cup, thinking, How will we get rich charging 25 cents? Splitting the proceeds with his sister meant only 12.5 cents per cup. Once his sister and he disagreed, there was no compromise. She taped her sign to a plastic bench. Nick made his own jug of lemonade and put a kitchen barstool with his sign—"Lemonade—$1"—right next to her table and was in business!

Needless to say, people were perplexed by the competing stands and pricing, but were impressed by Nick's assertion that his lemonade was worth a dollar. Sure enough, Nick sold more and made more money. This was his first real-world business lesson: there's more to business than price. If you can position a product in ways that appeal emotionally to consumers with a higher perceived value and deliver it to meet and ideally exceed expectations, they'll feel good paying whatever you charge. We teach team members the importance of giving clients the best experience possible. College Hunks Hauling Junk isn't the cheapest junk-removal company. But we brand ourselves and deliver an experience so that people agree that we're worth the extra dollars. And we are!

GREAT CLIENT SERVICE

A very high percentage of buying decisions are emotional and few are logical, according to statistics we've seen. Nick was a cute five-year-old selling lemonade for $1 so people bought from him. We tell team members the $1 lemonade story to illustrate the importance of providing clients with a remarkable *experience*. When people realized that Nick's lemonade was exactly the same as his sister's, they bought hers the second time around.

People pay more if there's a perceived superior value. The first time was emotional satisfaction from paying $1 to a greedy but cute entrepreneurial kid. But people wise up. If they can get the exact same product or service for less, and the experience is no different, they'll go for the lower price next time and advise friends to do the same. Starbucks charges much more for coffee than 7-Eleven. People who prefer the Starbucks experience and environment are willing to pay for it. If the experiences were exactly the same, no one would ever buy a Starbucks coffee.

When we started our business, we wanted to be a premier home service company, and we weren't the cheapest service. People loved our name, derived emotional satisfaction from hiring us, but also expected a better experience and more value, since we charged more. However, we got no repeat or referral business, because our service was no different from that of the guy in the pickup truck charging less. That's when we recognized the importance of giving clients a great experience. If we hadn't, we'd be out of business. The client experience determines whether they'll buy from you again or warn others that your lemonade isn't worth the price you're asking.

As an organization, we stopped referring to people who use our services as *customers*. They're now always referred to as *clients*, and our employees are referred to as *team members*. *Client* and *team member* reflect a higher level of importance and value to an organization than the antiquated terms *customer* and *employee*. Who would you rather be—somebody's customer or somebody's client? An employee or a team member? When we started looking at our clients and team members in this light, our attitude became all about satisfying people.

Develop staff, client, and community loyalty.

People had expectations when hiring us. If we didn't deliver, we were doomed. We made a point of creating a client service system that emphasized a superior and remarkable experience that's distinctly more enjoyable and memorable than what other junk haulers provide. Now not only do clients pay more for our services, but our repeat referral business has increased to 40 percent monthly. To accomplish this has meant focusing on whom we hire, team member training, and how we treat team members.

After enjoying an especially positive dining experience at a restaurant, where you're greeted by name, your water glass is refilled often, the waiter remembers what you ordered to drink last time, and you're treated like royalty by the manager, do you say, "I sure am satisfied," or do you say, "That was one of the best dining experiences I've ever had. I'm coming back often and telling all my friends." That's how we want our clients to feel about College Hunks Hauling Junk.

Your goal shouldn't be merely to satisfy your clients' needs. You want to leave them marveling about the level of service your brand delivered from start to finish. Everyone who has contact with a client or is involved with providing the service should be onboard with these efforts. A loyal client becomes a cheerleader for your company and wants your company to succeed. Figure out how to wow the customer at every interaction point. Everything should be a superb, unforgettable experience for clients, like the meal you want to have again and recommend to friends.

We ask clients what they like about the client experience. If we only meet their expectations, we'll go out of business. This won't generate repeat and referral business. If we exceed expectations, someone will do it better. If we AMAZE clients, they'll be so surprised they'll tell others. Never look at pricing as a strategic advantage over your competitor. Someone can always charge less. We wanted to compete on the value we provided to our client. We certainly are not the cheapest haulers but we provide a stressfree experience and premium service. This doesn't just start a conversation, where people ask us how we're different, and we explain why we're 20 percent more expensive; it also forces us to think strategically and figure out how to deliver more value. Now we sell lots of $5 lemonade and create high demand for it because of the overall experience, not just the surface value!

HIRING THE FIRST TEAM MEMBERS

Sam was the first team member to buy into our vision. When he rolled up in a white caddie with twenty-inch rims and tinted windows, we knew he would fit right in. Having him as a reliable captain and manager handling the day-to-day tasks helped us concentrate on growing the business in other areas. He's a perfect example of a team member who made the company vision his own and, in turn, defined his own vision as an entrepreneurial team member and used that to grow his department as if it were his business. Eventually, his role as manager reached a plateau. We had to make the painful decision to part ways. It's not easy to let go of someone who has been there since the beginning. It's literally like telling your college freshman roommate that you no longer need his friendship after graduation.

We had to hire staff to help the company grow. When recruiting front-line junk haulers or people to answer phones, we hired those who fit our client service criteria. But what about managers? People usually promote team members who've been loyal and with them the longest. This may seem logical, but ask yourself: Is this person qualified to help me grow my company? We made the mistake of promoting our friends' younger siblings as well as our early employees, assuming we could trust them in positions of authority. They did as they were told, but also took advantage of our relationship by showing up late or not at all.

The biggest challenge at the beginning was turnover. The days were interesting enough, but there were no incentives or camaraderie. Team members would meet the truck, do the jobs, and that was it. It wasn't even about getting the right people onboard.

It was a struggle to get people on the team, period. It quickly became apparent that we needed to learn how to get the right people or our client service standards would never be upheld. A successful leader finds those who love the mission and the work.

DELEGATING RESPONSIBILITY

When it was just the two of us, we goofed up but managed to get things done. Our team members screwed up worse. Usually, when things get tough in the business, entrepreneurs jump in and do everything themselves. But that's working harder, not smarter. We were stymied about how to delegate responsibility to others when they kept creating problems we had to clean up. Then we accepted that to build a successful business, you must also build a successful staff.

Create effective systems to keep your business on track and enable individuals to succeed.

If a team member came back with $300 in sales and $400 in disposal costs, and had a blank stare when asked why he bid the jobs so low, it wasn't his fault. It was our fault for not providing proper training, metrics, benchmarks, or infrastructure for him. When our business started to struggle, Nick considered moving back to D.C. from Tampa to help boost sales. But it would have been a Band-Aid, not a cure. The real problem was we didn't input accountabilities and hire superior talent. Nick put himself back into the fire to keep the business moving, on top of his other tasks.

This meant fifteen-hour days. Nick juggled more balls than one person should, and didn't focus on the more important tasks of systemizing the operation and leading his team to victory.

If your staff fails, it's because YOU failed to create efficient systems for them to follow and YOU didn't hire the right people or create the right hiring process for your management to hire them. When good systems are in place you can delegate work, which is essential to becoming an effortless entrepreneur. Getting started with delegation is challenging. Slowly delegate activities that keep you working IN the business and enlist input from your team to create systems that can improve the effectiveness of your business. This not only empowers them with a sense of contribution to the company, but also leverages their experience in the field and provides insights into how to do things more effectively and efficiently.

Nick's motto is "Delegate or die trying." If you don't, you'll burn yourself out of business. There are far too many things to be done within a business. It's a machine that's too complicated for one person to manage alone. As the owner, your primary role should be leading. To do that effectively, delegate the necessary action items on a day-to-day basis and delegate tasks to the management. Monitor the success and replication of those action items. Delegation is not an all-or-nothing proposition. There are four stages:

1. You assign a task, and your staff come back to report the outcome.
2. Your staff already know what they're supposed to do, but if anything comes up they ask you for direction.

3. Your staff know what they're supposed to do, and they will notify you if something comes up, but they will make recommendations instead of simply asking for direction.

4. You delegate tasks to your staff, giving them full authority, they know what they're accountable for, they do it, and they meet weekly for you to modify or reassign action items or priorities.

Work ON the business from the outside, not IN it.

Our biggest milestone was getting off the truck. There was no way our business would grow if we hauled junk every day. We quickly delegated that work. The next step was delegating management of our D.C. operations to Sam so we could focus on national expansion and franchising. When the D.C. performance suffered after we withdrew from daily management, we revisited the systems of daily truck team operation and management. It not only benefited that operation, but also helped our entire franchise network and positioned us to continue growing nationally. In addition to systemizing and delegating, we outsourced a lot of the key functions of our business, including PR, marketing, graphic design, accounting, and finance, until it made sense financially and strategically to bring those roles in house.

HIRING THE RIGHT PEOPLE

At first we promoted people from within, as most small businesses do. This backfired often. A year into the business we promoted a longtime hauler to weekend manager and celebrated having weekends off! Unfortunately, despite being a trustworthy hauler, he left work at 1 P.M. on a Saturday. Our phone rep reported that there were still clients needing service that day. Thankfully, the phone rep knew how to drive a truck and did the jobs himself. Because of his loyalty and initiative, it seemed obvious to promote the phone rep to weekend manager. Unfortunately, that backfired too. He threw temper tantrums—literally throwing chairs—and screamed in tears when he got fed up that haulers took advantage of him by showing up late or not listening to his instructions.

We had to reevaluate our entire hiring and manager-training process. The Peter Principle states that team members rise to their level of incompetence. The truth is they tend to be promoted for the wrong reasons. Trust is a critical factor for those you hire. Just as in a partnership, you must trust people who represent your business. Of course, loyalty and integrity are important, but a skill set is also needed. If you hire a manager with no management background, who has never hired, trained, motivated, or reprimanded a team, how effectively can he motivate and help grow your company? More important, how detrimental is that to long-term growth? You don't need to recruit a high-performing manager you can't afford. But give more consideration to the actual skill set one offers. Loyalty does not always signal competence. You need both.

There are always people smarter than you—hire them!

People who are smarter than you are an asset, not a threat. Assuming someone shares your goals, vision, and passion for the business and has appropriate motivational mechanisms in place, he'll help grow the business to the next level and uncover strategies and ideas you might not think of. A business owner should never promote or pay someone based on sheer effort. There *must* be performance-based benchmarks and measurable, attainable, and agreeable incentives. If someone isn't motivated by money or performance incentives, like trips or perks, that person won't add long-term value. She'll do the work until she gets bored or burns out, then move on.

Figure out how much someone needs for his lifestyle. Put a base salary in place that meets those needs, and have a bonus tied to growth in company revenue or profits. We spent six months deliberating on whom to hire as our national franchisee head coach. It was a crucial position that our franchisees' success depended on. We hired a younger guy with less experience but a proven track record in a high-growth start-up environment. His confidence resonated with us during the interview process when he said, "No one you hire will treat your business like you guys do, but I'm as close as they come to it." And he was right.

DEVELOPING STANDARDS OF ACCOUNTABILITY

To gain the absolute best value from team members, help them understand the importance of systems so they can write operating manuals, procedures, and checklists for you. They'll feel smart, important, and valued, and provide the backbone to build your standardized procedures. This helps you create the most successful systems. While you shouldn't tell team members this, the best part about having them help you create the standard procedures is that it helps you become less reliant on them. Having systems in place that your staff helped develop makes them more expendable if their performance goes down, since others could follow them if they falter.

We had an assistant manager who reached his ceiling and added no new value to the company. He seemed to be in a rut and stagnant in terms of productivity. Fortunately, he'd played a major role in helping create a system that made his tasks more efficient and easier to teach. When it was apparent he could no longer contribute to the company's growth, we replaced him with someone who did the exact same job for a fraction of the salary, since we had a more efficient system that could be followed. A rule of thumb for a business owner is "Be quick to fire, slow to hire."

Accountability keeps people honest and enforces the systems and performance-measurement tools you create. Just like goals, accountability should use the SMART method: standards should be specific, measurable, attainable, realistic, and timely. A team member's accountability should be answered with a simple *yes* or *no* when deciding whether that specific action item was completed or not. A salesman's accountability may be 5 percent annual new client growth. By the year's end, he's accountable for that metric. If he doesn't hit it, it's either step it up or step out.

Keeping someone on your team depends on your tolerance for misconduct or lack of performance. For us, anyone who doesn't uphold our core values is gone instantly. For a start-up, often it's the system that's flawed, not the individual. Reviewing accountability regularly forces a team member to do what's expected.

For example, we were losing many tools in the D.C. warehouse, so we made someone directly accountable for them. If they were lost, his paycheck was hurt. We didn't lose another tool after that. He implemented a system to prevent loss and made everyone accountable.

Mistakes are problems only if you do not learn from them.

A vendor once overcharged us for eighteen months and it cost nearly $50,000. We had to decide whether to give the team member responsible for the mistake a second chance. We told her it takes ten instances of flawless performance to erase one bad mistake. We wanted her to learn from her mistake and perform flawlessly going forward. She was unable to and we had to replace her. Similarly, we give front-line team members a $5 bonus for every compliment they receive and we deduct $50 for every complaint. This is because it takes ten happy clients to erase one unhappy client, since one happy client might tell one other person whereas one unhappy client will tell at least ten.

LEARNING TO FIRE

Ask any business owner about the toughest part of his job, and he'll say, "Employees." The problem is perspective. A team member doesn't see things the same way the owner does. You're the owner, therefore the bus driver. It's your job to drive that bus to reach your vision. Guess who's riding with you? You guessed it—your team members. They could be like highly caffeinated children, screaming and shouting, which distracts the driver from reaching the destination and can cause your bus to crash. Or they could be your eyes and ears, alerting you to things that could cause an accident.

You must create an environment with rules, but also make passengers want to help. Those who've been on the bus longer regulate newer riders. If someone steps out of line, they'll say, "We don't do things like that. It's like this." Your job is to get the right people on the bus and jettison the wrong ones. Sometimes you need to be tough. While second chances work, third and fourth chances are regrettable. During tough situations, everyone must pitch in. If there's dead weight onboard, cut it. It's critical to understand that the people you don't fire are the ones who will make your life miserable.

Firing a team member is a weird experience. While there are legal ramifications and instructions on how to properly let someone go, the process isn't simple, especially at a start-up. Often we wished for the nerve to fire someone as Donald Trump does on *The Apprentice*. Business textbooks advise writing someone up three times, keeping diligent team member files, and having another person present to witness the termination. But small businesses juggle many balls while getting started. It's hard to do everything by the book.

At first, firing people resembled dating patterns from school years. Over time, our techniques matured. Our first firing was similar to the awkward breakup of a first-time middle-school relationship. We literally stopped calling the team member to come to work, just as a young guy might ignore the girl he's dated, stop messaging her, and just hope she goes away. This team member had been with us for only three weeks. It was awkward and uncomfortable, but we didn't call him, and he never called us, which was a relief.

Our second firing was by phone. The team member had been with us for six months. Like the end of an unstable and immature six-month high school relationship, that firing was filled with drama. We tried letting him down easily, saying that his services weren't needed. He demanded a reason. We explained that he always arrived late and never wore his uniform properly. He screamed, threatened us, and called us for days before finally giving up.

Our third firing was of a one-year team member, similar to the first true love of an older high school student, and was filled with emotion. We gave him the "It's not you, it's me" speech and suggested he take a different direction in his career. He went from anger, to sadness, to begging to stay. The breakup, we mean firing, lasted hours until he finally accepted his fate.

The next firing was like telling a family member he was no longer wanted. After three years, his productivity had reached a lull while sales declined. Because he was one of our longest-tenured team members, firing him was a gut-wrenching two-month decision. The team member had seen it coming and bowed out gracefully. Slowly we got better at hiring, which made firing a less frequent occurrence. Once you play by the book more consistently, you can create systems that empower team members to make those decisions. The first manager we hired had a script and protocol to follow to fire someone, so it went smoothly.

If you dismiss someone for gross misconduct, ask yourself why this team member was hired in the first place. Most small-business owners mistakenly hire for convenience. The Peter Principle also applies when you promote for convenience. Emotion must be removed from all business decisions. Team members who hurt or just don't help the business must be cut. Speak with an employment-practices attorney or even an HR person from another company when creating your firing system. There are significant legalities involved. You can be sued for wrongful termination or discrimination if you don't follow proper legal protocol.

CREATING A COMPANY CULTURE

Before we understood the importance of having a company culture, we had significant negative employee activity. They stole from us. One broke into our office during the night to steal our company checks and credit cards. Employees showed up late, or not at all. Some quit in the middle of a day or refused to wear the company uniform properly. It was a huge headache.

Little things happened that we'd brush off: a careless truck accident, a client complaint, team members not showing up. Finally we realized that we had a bigger problem. One of our best team members called midday to quit, leaving two jobs hanging. He complained that his truck brought in thousands of dollars and he had nothing to show for it. We drove luxury cars because of his hard work and all the company cared about was making money. Hearing that felt like being punched in the gut.

Develop staff, client, and community loyalty.

Team members go through transitions: excitement on arrival, competency after three to six months, then boredom. They leave or step up to the next level, with new challenges and responsibilities. Like a kid with a new toy, everything is fun at first. We had a team member we'll call Mark who was excited about his job. Every house had something cool. He didn't mind hard jobs like cleaning out a compulsive hoarder's house with items piled up and rats under them, because they were unique experiences. Mark could go all day without checking with his manager. But after nine months he changed.

Mark acted entitled to infractions, since he'd "earned his stripes." He became a cancer, demoralizing new, excited recruits. It wasn't about money. Mark was no longer fulfilled by his role and suddenly quit. We hadn't asked him key questions, like What should we do as a company? Or stop doing? What works? We didn't create advanced responsibilities to make him feel smart, valued, and important. We were so engrossed in growing our company that we'd lost sight of what was happening around us.

We'd finally broken out of the nine-to-five prison and were free. Two twenty-three-year-old guys who grew up hating the system were no longer accountable to anybody—we *were* the system. We didn't work alongside team members as in the old days; we were the bosses. Our office was nicer, with top-of-the-line designer furniture. Our luxury cars glistened in the parking lot, vacations were more frequent, and we rarely interacted with team members. People we didn't even know worked for us. We became less aware of our surroundings and more focused on the future, growing sales, expanding, and generating PR. Then a sickening thought hit us: Our company was turning into everything we hated about the corporate world!

Veteran team members burned out and quit or became bitter. We were no longer fun-loving bosses who worked with our guys. We seemed like two stiffs working at a desk. How had this happened? Sure, we cared about making money, but we cared about much more than that. We envisioned creating a place to work that was different from what we'd experienced—a place that was fun, energetic, where team members were part of the business. Something had to change, but we didn't know what. At an entrepreneurs' conference we heard something that shook us to the bone. Most companies fail for one reason. They lack *company culture*. It made sense. If the customer service experience is the external reflection of a brand, and the employee experience is the internal reflection of a brand, the employee experience must be perfected to ensure that the client's experience is outstanding.

It's crucial to nurture relationships for the highest good of the company. We vowed to create an amazing company culture. Our motto became "Building leaders." Whether they planned to work for two months or two years, our team members would learn, grow, and become leaders. They were taught that their truck was their own small business. They controlled costs, sales, and profits. We implemented a profit-sharing program and overhauled the office, hanging photos resembling baseball cards of every team member. The frames listed their hobbies, favorite foods, and other personal characteristics.

Each team member got a business card with a link for clients to vote for team members who gave super service. We put rave client reviews under the photos. Monthly awards, such as "Truck Captain of the Month" and the "Git R Done" award for a team completing a difficult job, were presented during the relaxing atmosphere of the all-staff breakfast. We made it a point to have quarterly one-on-one reviews with each team member and to grade them on accountability. Pay raises were tied to performance reviews. Now we have monthly contests and awards. After being with the company for four years, employees get a custom letterman jacket with their name on it, helping create team spirit. We noticed a change immediately. All of a sudden we had an actual team of individuals working together rather than clock punchers.

It's crazy, but we realized that it wasn't monetary awards that team members cared about. They appreciated the emotional recognition. We expressed what we knew all along: They were the face of the company, the ones who determined the success of our brand. If they wanted to grow with us they could. College Hunks Hauling Junk was featured in *Washingtonian* magazine as one of the "City's Best Places to Work." We went from team members not lasting more than three months to celebrating two-, three-, and four-year anniversaries.

We have daily huddles that are essential to creating alignment and keeping your finger on the pulse of your business. It takes time, but once a rhythm is established, you create a culture of accountability and execution. The daily huddle should include:

- Good news
- Numbers and metrics (from the previous day)
- Where you are stuck (difficulties from the previous day)
- Your top priority for the day: if team members share their

"Top 1," they've been thinking about it; if they consistently can't share it, they probably shouldn't be there

Our daily huddle is at 11:11 A.M. At 11 A.M. people know to prepare. They write down good news, numbers they're account-able for, anything they're stuck on, and their Top 1 for the day. If we're out of town, we dial in. If we can't, the staff meets anyway. It creates alignment, keeps people thinking, and shows that your team is still proactive. Imagine a football team that never hud-dled before a play and didn't have practice or signals to properly execute a no-huddle offense. It would be completely ragtag and they'd get nothing accomplished.

One quarterly theme we use is called "Dish out the salt." Nick often says, "You can lead a horse to water but you can't make him drink . . . but you can give him a salt tablet to make him thirsty." Our teams were concerned that few franchise partners took ad-vantage of the great resources we provided. We made it a prior-ity to generate local publicity for our franchises. Then we mailed clips of the successful media hits received by those who used the resources to the other franchises owners, along with a salt packet, and wrote, "These articles could have been about your business if you had taken the time to use available resources." It was a huge success. We generated more than twenty local media hits in one quarter and made believers of all of our franchise partners.

Omar says that a company with no culture is like a frame with no picture. You can have all the systems in the world (your frame), but if there's no culture, you have an empty business. Team members won't follow systems. They'll quit and won't care about your vision. Find ways to recognize team members' accomplishments. Have contests. Praise them in a company newsletter. Display their photos and info about them. All of us want to feel valued for our efforts. Implementing a company culture creates a loyal and happy staff that will go the distance for your company and give clients the kind of experience that makes them return and refer you to others.

SYSTEMS FOR A SUPERIOR CLIENT SERVICE EXPERIENCE

To create a more enjoyable and memorable experience that encouraged repeat business and referrals, we defined our system on paper, listing all client interactions or "touch points." For us it's initial impressions, phone calls, truck team arrival, truck team interaction, and final follow-up. For each interaction, identify possible service defects, standards, opportunities to go above and beyond. Rank what's most important. Remember, each interaction provides an opportunity to wow your clients. Here are some of the standards we teach team members for impressing clients. Use our outline to create your own.

COLLEGE HUNKS HAULING JUNK CLIENT EXPERIENCE GUIDELINES

For a new client: This requires more education and value establishment from the truck team. The client is unfamiliar with our services, so it's important to describe them and build rapport before discussing pricing.

- Recognize that it's the client's first time. Act excited: "This is your first time? Welcome to the family!"

- Talk about college. "I'm currently in school at _____." Or "I'm taking a semester off from _____."
- Deliver exceptional experience, sweep up, thank the client for his business, and leave magnets and discount and vote cards.
- Ask for referrals.

For a repeat client or a returning client:

- Act excited to see her again: "Welcome back. Good to see you again."
- Deliver exceptional service, sweep up, thank her for repeat business, leave magnets and discount cards.
- Say "See you soon" when leaving.

We rank VIP clients and try even harder to keep them:

- Silver is a multiple repeat residential/commercial client.
- Gold is a regular repeat commercial/professional client that uses our services once a month.
- Platinum is a regular repeat commercial/professional client that uses our service more than once a month.

We teach mandatory standards to all team members, such as wearing the complete uniform with the shirt tucked in, calling before arrival, and many of the points listed above. Building people equity is a challenging, ever-evolving component of building a successful business. Nick envies his friend who owns an e-mail-marketing firm that does $10 million annual revenues with only four team members. But there's something to be said about the human element of working with people in a service business. More of our interactions these days are less personal because of technology. But running a business gives you an opportunity to create a new culture and grow something special, another bonus of playing the game.

CREATING COMMUNITY LOYALTY

The more you give back to your community, the more the community will support you. When you sponsor local events, your business name gets out in a memorable way. Find ways to get involved with community activities. Get the rest of your staff to donate time, money, or services where they're needed. Being involved in the community is fun and great for business. Instead of spending tons of money on advertising, donate your time to get your name out. Our franchises are encouraged to get involved in local activities, and they report favorable results.

We actually look for franchise partners who have lived in their territory for a substantial period and have strong community ties. We don't want someone who just wants to make money. We seek partners who want to make their neighborhoods, schools, and cities better places. We donate our trucks to can drives, cleanup efforts, and fund-raisers as much as possible. A portion of our sales goes to college scholarship funds that help inner-city kids get a four-year college education. Each year we present a student with a College Hunks Hauling Junk scholarship.

Technology and mass media have made the nation a smaller

place. We are all part of the community. As the recession proves, when the community struggles, everybody struggles. The more you can do for the greater good, the more you help yourself. Just as satisfied clients are your best salespeople, community service can create the kind of goodwill that brings clients in to at least check you out. Then you can wow them with an exceptional experience and turn them into cheerleaders for your company.

CHAPTER 8

EVOLUTION OF A BRAND
Standing Out in a Crowded Landscape

There's an old trick some guys use to pick up girls—they "show out" by dressing as flashily as possible to attract attention, like male birds with bright, flashy feathers. Many women are attracted to the brightest, most in-your-face personality in the bar or club. To test this theory, we went out wearing all white—linen pants, shirts, and Kangol hats. We looked like we belonged in a drug cartel in Colombia, but lo and behold, it made us the center of attention at the bar, on the street, and in the clubs. We literally caused a traffic jam as cars stopped and tried to figure out who we were and why we were dressed like Don Corleone or for a P. Diddy white party in the Hamptons. We had no problem talking to girls that night and came home with many phone numbers. Showing out at clubs is similar to showing out in business.

A brand must stand out. Every day Nick passes a corner where people collect money in buckets for charities. Only an occasional motorist contributes. Yet when firefighters collected money, people gave like crazy. They looked good, like stereotypical firefighters on a calendar, and ran from car to car as people waved dollars at them. Nick realized why. They raised money for a cause people believe in *and* looked the part. This works for us too. People like supporting college students, and our guys look the part. If the firefighters were fifty-year-olds with huge guts, the reaction would be very different. We think this is part of consumer psychology. Image is critical to consider as part of a growth strategy.

FAKE A MULTIMILLION-DOLLAR IMAGE TILL YOU MAKE IT

We maintain the same mentality used to improve our personal lives as we develop an image to advance our company. In a competitive marketplace, it helps to stand out. There are always barriers to getting in contact with a bigwig you want to connect with or a commercial prospect you want to sell to. With the right persona and words defining our image, our personal victories taught us how to succeed in business. Fake the success you intend to have until you make it!

Start with a vision, create a strategic plan, and live by it.

Since day one, we talked and acted like a multimillion-dollar operation, in the same brazen way we crashed parties and sports events. People do believe the hype. The best way to turn hype into reality is to live it. Your company is only as good as how people perceive it. If you make a good impression, you'll attract more clients, and vendors will be more likely to work well with you. That's why it's important to create the most professional, impressive facade you can get away with. Don't blatantly lie or mislead people into believing that you're something you are not. Simply position yourself as a company that walks, talks, and acts like the one you created in your long-term vision for the company.

Visualize the company you want to become, then act the part, and you'll eventually grow into the image. We used the same guerrilla tactics that got us into doors in our personal lives to put our business on the map. Instead of trying to open resistant front doors, we would sneak in the back door. For example, we helped build College Hunks Hauling Junk as a household name and part of pop culture by getting onto a prime-time ABC reality TV show that featured our concept. That resulted in numerous offers related to our business brand. We're now sneaking through the back door in Hollywood in the same way. The more you create a good brand and put it brazenly in people's faces, the greater the chance of your company becoming successful.

Image is everything.

From the beginning we created the impression of being a national company, though we were far from that. Remember, we were twenty-two-year-old guys with no experience running a business when we began to operate College Hunks Hauling Junk. Our budget was tight. We ran around doing everything ourselves and hired friends to help with big jobs. Our first office was a mess. But it didn't show in our image. Even when we had just one truck, people said, "Your company is a franchise, right?" or "You guys are really growing!" We'd let them know we were not yet, but would be soon. Sharing our vision of growth with clients inspired them to believe in us and want us to grow as well.

The image you project to the public creates the initial perception of your business. From the beginning we created a fake roster of staff members so people wouldn't perceive us as a ragtag operation. Initially, there were three such "employees": Nicolette Marquetti was director of PR, Jason Miller was customer service representative, and Robby Martin was marketing director. We created e-mail addresses for them: PR@1800JunkUSA .com, service@1800JunkUSA.com, and marketing@1800Junk USA.com, though in fact it was just us checking the e-mails.

We'd e-mail prospective clients using these addresses to make ourselves seem bigger, knowing that eventually these positions would be filled by someone else. Omar pitched a story to the *Washington Post* from PR@1800JunkUSA.com and signed it Nicolette Marquetti. Eventually, the reporter wanted to do the piece and thought he was coordinating with Nicolette to set up the interview with Omar. In reality he was working with Omar the entire time. Such ruses made people more comfortable dealing with us as a business.

Find ways to present a professional persona for your company from the beginning. Our methods weren't designed to be deceitful. We just knew that people, especially commercial clients, preferred doing business with larger, more professional companies. Our Web site was cutting-edge, our trucks were branded, and our uniforms were clean and crisp. So even as rookies, our outward appearance was that of a polished and seasoned business. Sure enough, two years later we had people in all those positions and our company was more like we had presented it from day one.

WINNING WITH YOUR FIRST IMPRESSION

You'd dress appropriately for a job interview—well groomed from head to toe. When you own a business, approach your image as if you were on a 24/7 job interview. First impressions are everything. Unfortunately, people don't have time to get to know you, so they make most assumptions based on what they see in the first few seconds. We wanted to ensure that our first impressions made the greatest impact on clients. When we answered the phone we said, "Thanks for calling College Hunks Hauling Junk. How can I help you have a junk-free day?" This usually got a laugh and broke the ice.

We learned a lot about the importance of making a good first impression while we were trying to pick up girls, and we brought those lessons into our company to help develop our image. Both sexes have a higher success rate for attracting someone to date when their image is appropriate for their goals. We learned to tell which girls wanted to meet someone for a long-term relationship and who were only looking for some fun. It's not just about outside appearance, though this is very important. It's also about your message and how your carry yourself. We wear our khakis and College Hunks Hauling Junk shirts for many activities, but also know when a suit is appropriate.

Confidence creates the best image for business or pleasure. You never want to seem desperate. Even if you're very attracted to someone you meet, it's best to approach her in a confident way. This is what you should do with a potential client whose business you want badly as well. Your demeanor should make it clear that even if you're turned down, it won't be the end of the world, since there are other people to date and other clients to sign. This actually makes you more attractive because people want goods and services, and to date people, that others also want. None of us wants to feel as if we ended up with someone who was just desperate for any action at all.

It's natural for people to struggle with their confidence when it comes to picking up women or men, and the same goes for promoting your brand. The only way to improve is to keep doing it and stretch your comfort zone. The key word for the confidence you need is *swagger*—carrying yourself with an air of self-assurance that screams that you believe in the value of your business and yourself. It takes practice:

- Practice introducing yourself to people.
- Practice making eye contact.
- Practice standing tall and confidently.
- Practice smiling without looking silly.
- Practice forgetting about failures or misses by focusing on your belief in yourself and the future success you're going after.

It's the same for a company's brand. When potential clients saw we didn't give a hard sell, they assumed we were doing well, which made a good impression. Buying our Range Rover and having a professional demeanor that reflected assurance helped convey that we weren't desperate kids trying to make some money. It gave the impression that we were leaders with real confidence in our own business. That made us more attractive than if we'd looked like a crappy bush-league operation, just offering any potential client a crazy good deal out of desperation.

It could really be useful for you to think of a potential client as someone you'd like to pick up. It can get you thinking in terms of what a client is looking for and how to create a company image that will respond to those needs. Just as we dressed in different ways to pick up different kinds of girls, your brand should reflect your goals and what would best appeal to your target audience. If you're looking to meet a simple old-fashioned girl or guy, or your company is targeting family-oriented clients, a high-rollers' approach, like ours with the Range Rover, probably isn't right for you. Just as in dating, a good and appropriate image gets you the first opportunity to make your pitch. Then your sales skills come into play to get the person hooked for the sales pitch, and ultimately to make the sale (more on this in chapter 10).

Develop staff, client, and community loyalty.

Our team members are trained to shake hands with clients on arrival and introduce themselves with their name and what college they attend. They're taught to speak clearly and politely and to always make eye contact. Uniforms are always neat, with shirts tucked in. No trash company in the world brings our level of service. It's fueled our rapid growth. Our best promoters are satisfied customers whom we convert into loyal clients. They become cheerleaders, brand ambassadors promoting our service to others. People gravitate to a trusted brand and are more likely to buy from a company with a good reputation.

Image is hard to maintain. When we moved our headquarters to Tampa, we returned to D.C. months later to find our operation in a very unsavory condition. Trucks were dirty, misused, and damaged, their paint and logos scratched. Team members and managers weren't tucking in their shirts or presenting the clean-cut image we'd left behind. We had to rebuild a level of pride and accountability in the operation. It's also difficult to teach an old dog new tricks. At first, we hadn't defined all the brand standards and image requirements of staff, so guys who were with us from the very beginning were difficult to convert to new uniform requirements.

There's always room for a service or product that's branded well; people will want to try it. Omar jokes that he originally got the idea to do junk removal from a friend who was also doing it, whom we called "Rooster." After we started College Hunks Hauling Junk, Rooster fussed about our stealing his idea. By that logic, McDonald's stole the idea to sell hamburgers from every independent hamburger stand. But junk removal existed long before Rooster. Forget the Roosters who tell you your idea has already been done. Make it better!

STANDING OUT

Many business owners are afraid their company will be invisible and people won't notice it. Successful entrepreneurs channel those fears into creating a remarkable brand and giving service that stands out and gets noticed. From the beginning, our goal as a company has been to stand out in a crowded landscape and distinguish ourselves in a competitive field by providing tangible (the service and products) and intangible (creating an experience) things about College Hunks Hauling Junk that no other company had.

When others provide the same products and services you want to offer, it can seem impossible to make a place for yours. But you can. The most important part of setting up a business is identifying your core client and how what you'll offer is different. Otherwise you're just a "me too" business. There's NO company like College Hunks Hauling Junk, with the quality of the collegiate client service experience we offer. But there are tons of junk-hauling companies. If you can leverage an uncommon benefit, you can shine in any crowded landscape. A perfect example is Five Guys, a rapidly growing burger chain. It's remarkable that it can compete with McDonald's and Burger King. It does so by differentiating itself, appearing as not just another burger place, and by providing an overall experience that's completely different from other burger chains'.

As we grow, we continue looking for ways to deliver memorable service. We create an emotional response in people's minds by conveying the kind of experience they remember so well when they see our Web site or trucks, that they wouldn't consider another company. Our goal is to inspire people to buy from us. Our business concept is as simple as it gets. While we're not reinventing the wheel, we are reinventing its presentation. We saw a demand for the service, recognized that the human interaction experience could be improved, and did our best to improve it tenfold.

Seth Godin's book *Purple Cow* talks about being remarkable in business and standing out in a crowd. The idea is that if you drove down a street and saw a field full of brown cows, you wouldn't notice one. But if you saw a purple cow among them, you'd stop, look, and be intrigued. Our brand—bright orange-and-green trucks with a giant hunk holding the words *College Hunks*—is so out there and in-your-face that everyone notices. It may even offend some people. You must get people talking. Godin says if you don't offend someone, you're not doing enough. He also emphasizes that while you need a remarkable brand, it's more important to have a remarkable service or product that keeps people coming back and talking.

Ideas mean nothing without actions.

Looking flashy or out there may get you into a conversation. But if you don't wow the person with your words and what's experienced during your interaction, there's zero chance of winning the person over, let alone getting referrals. It was difficult for us to recognize that we needed to provide both a standout brand and a remarkable experience. We got the brand right at first, which is half the battle. But we fell flat when it came to the other half. While you may have some early success with just a flashy brand, if you disappoint clients with the overall experience, your business won't grow, and nothing will make up for a lousy product.

At first, when people called they got an unprofessional voice mail or an unscripted sales pitch from whoever answered. We stumbled through our words to explain how our service worked. We showed up out of uniform—in jeans, tennis shoes, T-shirts—looking ragtag. There was no system to follow that ensured a memorable experience to inspire them to recommend us to others. We'd quote a price without establishing a rapport. It took time to realize that the true future of our business wasn't in one-night stands. We needed a loyal base of repeat and referral business. Having that carried us through the economic downturns.

If you don't live up to your brand image, clients become upset. They'll be completely disappointed if what they expected doesn't happen. The double-edged sword with our business is that "college hunks" sets the bar high for what clients imagine. They expect a good-looking young college male. So our biggest challenge has been to position our brand in a way that delivers an overall experience that doesn't disappoint, even if the team member isn't in college or, worse, is unattractive. Our goal is focused around our core client. We don't target clients who just want eye candy, which is too limiting. Instead, we want people who think the idea is catchy and are inspired by having enthusiastic, friendly, and hardworking teams remove items from their home or office.

The emotional experience we provide is the satisfaction of interacting with and helping out hardworking men and women and the confidence of knowing their items are being taken care of responsibly. The power of an eye-catching, attention-getting business name can't be overemphasized. It's helpful to have one that makes people stop and look at it, ask questions, or joke about it. We get jokes all the time. Our name works as a magnet for the news media, which attracts publicity for the business.

Godin reminds us that if every cow becomes purple, a purple cow is no longer remarkable. This is inevitable. You always need to innovate, re-create, and try to keep a step ahead of people who try to imitate and mimic your keys to success. Our core purpose as a company is to "stay fresh." We want to stay at the forefront of people's minds and don't want to be lumped among all the other companies out there. Choose a brand name people will remember and find ways to make it scream so potential customers notice it. Then captivate those initial customers to make them brand evangelists who'll spread your gospel. Define what differentiates you from the competition and empower your clients to broadcast it louder to a more influential group, even if your competitors sell similar goods or provide similar services.

At College Hunks Hauling Junk our slogans help define how we operate. We use the slogan "America's Junk Removal Specialists" to establish ourselves as the premier national service. Other slogans are tied to our core values, such as "Making Green Look Good" and "Let Tomorrow's Leaders Haul Your Junk Today!" Creating taglines that fit with our core values as a company and branding ourselves with them compels us, along with our franchisees and staff, to strive to walk the walk of our brand promise every day.

DEVELOPING THE BRAND

Creating our logo was painstaking. We went back and forth for weeks, making over a hundred revisions in size, color, and imagery. We started with a simple logo from an online company. If you use a logo service, get the version with unlimited revisions. The original options were extremely bad—we mean horrible. Countless hours were spent deliberating and debating about which version we liked better, down to every tiny detail, including if the hunk should have rounded or angled eyebrows.

We presented the options to a panel of our peers and prospective clients to gauge their response, and the logo continued to evolve. A shaded orange was added behind the hunk to make the colors pop more on materials with our logo. Evolution is natural. FedEx's brand and logo have come a long way since the company was known as Federal Express. Ours has been evolving since day one. Our bright image has been a major factor in our success because it reflects our culture. The orange and green color scheme is fun, collegiate, and unique. In a way it looks like something a kid drew in his dorm room. People are attracted to it. A search engine optimization expert suggested that we revise our Web site because it looked amateurish, like a college kid designed it. He probably didn't realize that our company culture and brand *are* collegiate. That's the exact experience we want to give our Web site visitors!

Originally we liked the orange and green because they're the colors of the University of Miami, where we won the business-plan competition and our original idea was crafted. Now we say that orange represents our bright, playful brand, and green represents our recycling and environmentally friendly hauling practices. Be creative about how your brand plays to the public and the significance of the color scheme, logo, and message. Think about the emotional response people might have to it. Consider the differences in what people think of when they see Target's logo compared to Walmart's, or Best Buy's compared to Radio Shack's. They both provide essentially the same products, but the response to each of these brands is directly tied to the experience of walking into the stores. One might seem vibrant and fun; the other dull.

When we first launched, we struggled about how to position our Web site and phone number. Our original Web site was www. CollegeJunk.net and our number was 1-888-We-Junk-U. Neither fit our vision of becoming a national brand. We spent lots of time searching for available domain names and seeing who owned existing ones. We obtained the original phone number from Toll FreeNumbers.com, which allows you to search for available novelty numbers. However, we knew we needed something with more power to become a national brand.

Our Web site became www.1800JunkUSA.com, to fit with the phone number. CollegeHunksHaulingJunk.com seemed too long for someone to type, and CollegeHunks.com might have been mistaken for a porn site or something similar. Our 800 number did its job. People asked us if we were a national franchise when our business was still the two of us and one truck. The number implied that we had locations in other cities, while we still parked the truck at our parents' houses. But even to this day, we debate about whether our brand would benefit by going back to College-HunksHaulingJunk.com as our main Web site, with an abbreviation as our e-mail so it's easier to type.

PROTECTING YOUR BRAND

When we first launched our business, we were paranoid about someone stealing our name. College Hunks Hauling Junk was part of the magic surrounding our vision for the future. Omar tried to register it on the Web site for the U.S. Patent and Trademark Office (USPTO.gov), but it was rejected initially. Trademarks may not be approved if the name sounds more like descriptive words. We refused to be deterred, since we needed the name to build our national brand. We knew little about trademarks, but knew we needed one.

Fortunately, we did a junk-removal job for a trademark attorney and hired her. While pricey, a good attorney is a necessary asset. We couldn't counter the rejection of our name as a trademark, but our attorney did! It's easy and inexpensive to register a trademark yourself. We paid $250 and then another $1,500 for the attorney to get it approved. Since then we've spent over $150,000 registering and protecting ours. As we grew, our attorney advised us to register a combination of names, logos, and slogans to have a series of trademarks for more protection against copycats or parasite companies trying to benefit from our brand reputation. We also registered our slogans. The registered trademarks came in handy when companies imitated our brand and caused confusion in the marketplace.

A company with a similar name can make consumers think it's your company. For example, in the movie *Coming to America*, there's McDonald's and the fictional McDowell's. According to the owner of McDowell's, McDonald's has golden arches and the Big Mac. McDowell's has golden arcs and the Big Mic. Both have all-beef patties, with the same fixings, except McDonald's uses sesame-seed buns but McDowell's buns have no seeds. These differences are supposed to counter the similarities. Of course, in real life, McDonald's would never allow a company with such a similar name and product line to co-opt its brand, since it would dilute the value of the McDonald's brand and reputation. Our expectations were no different. You must stop brand copycats in their tracks or your business equity suffers.

Our first challenge came when students who had seen Omar's business plan win the competition tried to launch an online auction site with a similar name. We nearly freaked out because this concept had been in Omar's plan. While that company failed for the same reasons we'd chosen not to do it, we spent thousands to consult attorneys. Next a large Canadian company registered the domain JunkHunks.com and marketed a junk-removal calendar. The wind was knocked out of our sails, since we couldn't afford to pursue any more trademark protection at the time. Later, when that company reached out to us to request that we not sell a franchise to one of its employees, we got the domain names transferred to us as part of the agreement. You've got to be creative about protecting your brand when funds are low.

Brand thieves abound. When Omar called a former vendor, his voice mail said, "You've reached Strong Students Junk Removal." We couldn't believe it! He'd worked on our Web site, then used our collegiate junk haulers idea. A mentor advised us to call him directly, say he'd crossed the boundaries of trademark infringement, and suggest that he purchase one of our franchises. Sure enough, when Nick suggested that he could benefit from our brand, systems, support, and national brand presence, he jumped right in, and now he is one of our most successful and dynamic franchise owners. He'd hit a wall and was running himself ragged. The idea of aligning with a national support infrastructure appealed to him.

Over the years we've spent hundreds of thousands of dollars

to enforce our trademark whenever a parasite copycat company has tried to ride our coattails by confusing clients with similarities to our company. We've learned that it's very important to settle legal matters quickly; if you delay, the attorneys will win the most, while you'll spend hundreds of thousands of dollars and lots of energy with little to show for it. Talk to a good lawyer to make sure you're covered. Plan for potential infringements. Trademark all relevant names to put a wide circle of protection around your brand, but don't go crazy at the beginning if you're strapped for cash. Be vigilant. Do occasional searches on the Internet for copycats. The longer you allow one to operate with a business name, concept, or slogan that infringes on yours, the harder it is to stop him.

PRACTICING GUERRILLA AND TARGETED MARKETING

Develop staff, client, and community loyalty.

Our industry is very crowded, since anyone with a truck can haul junk. So we created a white-glove service concept to become the Ritz-Carlton of trash by focusing on customer service and being far superior to other junk-hauling services. Ritz-Carlton is known for its wow factors and superb reputation. When you strive to be the best company in your industry and do whatever it takes to be known for giving the greatest customer service possible, you have the best shot at building your own little Ritz-Carlton type of reputation. That attracts more customers!

Be the best at ONE thing.

The value of marketing and public relations can't be understated. If your business isn't based on a novel idea or a unique product— and hauling junk certainly isn't—marketing becomes the make or break element of the business—your secret sauce. We excelled beyond our expectations. A creative marketing concept is a very important element of success, particularly when you're entering a crowded marketplace. Adding an uncommon spin to a product or service makes it stand out. That's why video games keep getting reinvented. Add a new twist to the plot, and more bells and whistles, and people want that too, even if they have lots of games already. Creativity creates a "gotta have it" factor.

Image is everything.

A rule of thumb in marketing is "seven impressions," meaning someone needs seven encounters with your brand before he becomes a buyer, even the mayor of Washington, D.C. When Mayor Adrian Fenty ran for office, he knocked on doors and commented on the College Hunks Hauling Junk sign in Nick's front yard. One of our core values is always branding, so our signage and logo are plastered wherever possible. Nick assured Fenty that he had Nick's vote as long as he helped the new business get city contracts. They laughed. Months later, Nick went to an awards gala for College Bound, a charity we support. Mayor Fenty was the guest of honor. As always, Nick wore his green College Hunks Hauling Junk polo to the event. Mayor Fenty saw the logo and instantly remembered the lawn sign when they'd met at his house.

Three months later, Nick was at a Washington Redskins game and saw the mayor and his entourage. He ran up, handed him his business card, and said, "College Hunks Hauling Junk. Good to see you again." Months later Nick and his guerrilla marketing team went to a fall fair with the company mascot, CJ the College Junk Hunk. Mayor Fenty was there. He saw the mascot, said, "I see your trucks everywhere," and posed for a photo op with the mascot. The following summer we were hauling junk for the D.C. government.

Catchy marketing and unique angles aren't enough to create longevity and sustainability as a business. You must stay fresh to avoid being a flash in the pan or being made obsolete by new companies. A targeted marketing approach became much more vital once the economy started going down. During a good economy all it took was mass marketing, which we called "spray and pray." We spent money on marketing and prayed it would work, with little or no way to measure its success. But our target buyer became a more limited segment once budgets got tight, making the shotgun approach to marketing ineffective. Forcing ourselves to become better businessmen, we defined exactly who our ideal client was, by using surveys and creating different client lists based on profile, type, age, and demographic. We target potential clients with pinpoint accuracy through e-mails, direct mail, and other media.

A good Web site is an important investment, even if you're short on cash. People judge a business by its online face. There are great Web designers (especially in India) who can design your Web site for $10 an hour instead of the $300 hourly rate that large U.S. design firms might charge. The key is to make sure it looks as polished and professional as any S&P 500 company's Web site, which is definitely possible. Identify Web sites you like as a reference for the designer but don't copy them verbatim. Your content is specific to your business. Keep it updated, and keep it fresh!

GOING GREEN

We chose to go green as a company. Everything our trucks collect is disposed of using environmentally conscientious systems we created. We didn't decide to do this just to sound good. We want to walk the walk. In part, this is a contribution to the communities we serve. Companies around the world look for opportunities to go green. We knew this and thought, Here we are in a garbage-disposal industry and we're not taking full advantage. So we made this a focus.

Instead of hiring an expensive consulting company to design our green initiatives, we hired a university's senior PR class to work this concept as a case study. Our total cost was $500 for miscellaneous supplies and research. The students delivered an actionable game plan to execute our new slogan, "Making Green Look Good." We partnered with a national organization that had a database for all nonprofits and recycling facilities to use the resources more efficiently and seamlessly. Company material is printed on recycled paper. We publicize the percentage of junk we divert from the junkyard for good use. To measure how many items can be kept out, we created an intracompany competition to see which location recycled the most.

Develop staff, client, and community loyalty.

Doing good for the community, whether by volunteering, donating, or protecting the environment, is just another way to set your business apart from others and develop a loyal following of influencers who help grow your brand. It's also nice not to lose sight of the fact that we're all part of this world, and entrepreneurs have the greatest opportunity to make a difference in it. We need to do our part to make it a more inhabitable and enjoyable place for everyone. Initially, it was more expensive to recycle everything. We paid to dispose of items. It took more time and cost more to have teams separate and donate or recycle items we removed. Eventually, experts in logistics helped us make it work financially and environmentally. The majority of what we collect goes to donation or recycling facilities. The remainder is disposed of in environmentally friendly ways.

MARKETING YOUR BRAND WISELY

Marketing can be a mystery, but when measured and executed effectively it can be extremely scientific. If there were a magic switch that could be flipped to make clients walk through the door and purchase, many more start-up businesses would succeed. In reality, it's hard to predict what will yield a positive return. Traditional mass media advertising—television, radio, and print—are becoming outdated and overpriced. Without a mammoth marketing budget, these outlets won't work for your business.

Mistakes are problems only if you do not learn from them.

Initially, we spent money on all sorts of marketing: direct mail, $3,000; coupon savers, $1,000; local newspaper, $500 per month; major newspaper, $1,600 per month; online Yellow Pages, $1,600 per month; radio, $5,000 per campaign; TV, $3,000 per campaign. The cost far outweighed the number of clients we gained as a result. True, people do see ads, which creates another impression for your brand. But there are much less costly strategies. Many start-ups waste too much on marketing. Be careful about splurging on marketing ideas that sound cool but may not work.

As we said, there's a big difference between investments and expenses. When we started, everyone and his mother advised us to do a College Hunks Hauling Junk calendar. It seemed like a cool idea. When we had extra cash, we made one. This has been our biggest marketing flop. It cost a week of time to plan and $15,000 for photography, graphic design, and printing. We printed five thousand calendars and had nothing to do with them. People don't use calendars as much as they used to. Worst of all, they had a limited shelf life, since they'd be obsolete at the end of the year. So we mailed them to clients, which cost several thousand dollars more. We used photos from the shoot for other ads and on our Web site to make the most of this expenditure. Still, it was a money burn. But we chalked it up as a good idea gone bad. Had we analyzed the ROI, we'd have known it wasn't a wise investment.

One of our core values is "Always branding," and we live by this daily. We wear our College Hunks Hauling Junk polos whenever we travel in an airport or shop on weekends. It automatically creates a buzz or conversation. We brand our personal vehicles and our trucks. We put signs out around town to create constant reminders. Part of the fun of being a creative brand is doing these kinds of grassroots marketing and guerrilla marketing activities. We created a mascot costume for community events and developed relationships with area nonprofits for fund-raisers and co-promotions.

Our most memorable promotion by far was during the 2009 presidential inauguration in Washington, D.C. We took CJ the College Junk Hunk to Georgetown to attract attention. Omar put the costume on and walked around, but people ignored him. So we tried another approach—a truck parade to get our brand in front of people. We loaded all eight of our trucks, and Omar stood on top of the toolbox on the front truck in the mascot suit. He held on for dear life as our trucks drove through the most heavily trafficked pedestrian shopping area in the city in bumper-to-bumper traffic while hundreds of thousands of people pointed, cheered, and took photos of Omar waving.

"I felt like a rock star!" Omar exclaimed when it was over. Hundreds of people snapped pictures with cell phones and cameras. They'd never seen something like it. If this had been in a TV commercial, people would have ignored it, as they do when exposed to that type of advertising. But this was something different, something new, which they had not seen before. It created buzz. We expected the same result when our trucks drove through New York City's Times Square. But this crowd was immune to that sort of marketing. New Yorkers see it all—the good, the bad, and the freakish. The bright billboards in the city dwarfed our orange and green College Hunks Hauling Junk trucks. It taught us that we have to reevaluate our strategy in that environment.

You must study your market and learn what people will and won't pay attention to. Be aware of strategies that other businesses use and figure out the right ones for your business. Traditional forms of marketing and mass media (Yellow Pages, TV, radio, print ads) are in many cases becoming obsolete, while Internet marketing, such as search engine optimization (generic search results) and search engine marketing (pay-per-click advertising), is becoming more powerful and cost-effective. The best marketers for your business are still your clients. As you find ways to get your brand in front of the people most likely to buy your products or use your services, your client base will grow and, with it, your business.

GETTING MEDIA COVERAGE

Media coverage provides exposure for your business. Being written about in publications and interviewed on radio and television gives your company credibility, which is especially helpful in the early stages. Seeing your name in print or on television makes you feel good about your accomplishments. If you allow the publicity to create momentum rather than create a false sense of achievement, it can be a very powerful vehicle for marketing. You can hire a publicist or obtain media lists online and send press releases yourself. Sometimes you can find a good intern to make calls.

The secret of PR is that every journalist and reporter wakes up each morning needing something to report on. Guess what! You can do them a favor by providing them with that compelling, unique, informative story. You need one that the media find interesting. Don't just send a release saying you exist. If your business has an interesting angle, as ours did, use that. Or do something that might get you exposure, like charity work and getting involved in your community.

Position yourself as an expert in your industry or field. Then develop your target pool of reporters and journalists who cover your story type, just as you'd develop your target pool of prospective clients. When you have an interesting story, let the media know. Make phone calls and send e-mails. Call reporters and say, "Hi, this is _____. Do you have a moment? I've got a great story for you." Ask questions, listen for their needs, and respond accordingly. If you don't hear back, follow up, but not too frequently or you'll scare them away, just as you would an A client. You can build relationships with the media the way you do with your clients and become a valuable resource for them.

If the media call, be prepared to do what they need. It's often last-minute. Agree to a request and then figure out how to make it happen. Producers for *The Oprah Winfrey Show* called to ask if we had an operation in New York City. Nick quickly responded, "Of course! What do you need?" They wanted a truck and a team of hunks to film an episode two days later. "No problem," said Nick, and called Omar. "The good news is we'll be on TV. The bad news is we need a truck and two hunks in New York in two days or we'll ruin our chance of being on the show ever again. I said we had a truck there." Omar exclaimed, "But we don't have a location in New York yet!"

But when Oprah calls, you drop everything. Our most reliable team member, Sam, and his wingman, Josh, drove a Hunk truck from D.C. to meet Nick in New York. In showbiz things often don't go as planned. What started as one-day job turned into a weeklong project. Nick, Sam, and Josh stayed with friends in New York, sleeping on the floor, and shuffling to find parking for the Hunk truck, piling up parking tickets totaling over $1,000. But the reward was sweet when we heard from everyone who saw us on *The Oprah Winfrey Show*!

The media can be leveraged to expand your brand, but it's a challenge to keep a level head, as media exposure can make you think you're better than you actually are. It's easy to buy into the hype of your business and become complacent and lazy. Focus on staying hungry and humble. We reminded ourselves that we wanted a successful business, not just media success. Continue to focus on your actual product or service, your core customer, and how you provide that product or service to him.

When we hired a PR team to assist the franchisees with local publicity, we made the mistake of not teaching the franchisees how to do it themselves in the process. One of our locations experienced a 40 percent increase in sales when an article came out, but could never replicate that until we taught the franchisee how to do it effectively. For the secret to the College Hunks Hauling Junk publicity buzz and to download free press release and media alert templates as well as best practices for generating publicity for your business, go to www.effortlessentrepreneur.com.

CHAPTER 9

GENERATION TEXT
New Technology Meets a Traditional Business

Nick texted Omar that he was up to his ears in frustration about whether a team member (we'll call him Chris) was cut out for the job. Later Nick pulled out his cell phone, intending to text Omar one final complaint about Chris. But inadvertently, he selected Chris's name instead of Omar's, and texted the following:

Bottom line, Chris is incompetent. He doesn't see the big picture and comes in late every day. And it's like pulling teeth to get him to bid jobs properly.

A split second after Nick hit Send, he realized his error. We'd been talking about Chris so much that Chris's name was on Nick's mind, so Nick sent the message to him. There was nothing Nick could do. A text message can't be rescinded once you send it. Chris was working that day and was puzzled to receive the message. Nick immediately sent a follow-up message to Chris pretending like he was joking:

Ha-ha! LOL, just messing with you. But seriously, we're making a big emphasis on timeliness and sales goals.

It was a poor attempt to redeem himself. The damage was done. Chris knew how we felt about him and working with him became awkward. But he stayed. We were too embarrassed to fire him. He probably knew this, and his poor performance continued. Finally, we let him go, since there was no other choice, and we'd gotten over our texting embarrassment. We learned that electronic technology must be used carefully in business.

In 2004, a relatively unknown search engine company called Google went public. In less than three years it became the world's biggest media company (by stock value). Apple wasn't in the music-distribution business until 2003. With the creation of the iTunes Web platform, Apple is the number-one music retailer in the country. If this doesn't set off bells for a business owner, she has missed the bus. It's the beginning of the end for traditional media. Businesses that strategically take advantage of the digital age will ride the wave of success into the future. Those that don't will be swallowed whole.

CONNECTING WITH THE ELECTRONIC GENERATION

"Uh, I don't own a home phone," nearly 90 percent of our team members responded when we attempted to get their home info. Most of our team members are under twenty-five and grew up with technology glued to their fingers. Why would they own a piece of outdated equipment connected to a wall if something that performs the same function is in their pocket? With the surge in technology, romance for this generation begins with a serenade of text messages, Facebook pokes, MySpace comments, and the like. When do we pick up the phone and say, "Hey, how's it going? Would you like to have dinner with me?" Yikes! That's way too personal and leaves too much room for failure.

We came up with the name *generation text* after the fourth team member in a row texted us an hour before work that he couldn't come in. We were twenty-three-year-olds but sounded more like our grandparents: "What the hell's wrong with kids today?! They don't have the courtesy to call when they can't come in?! This is the #%# text-message generation!" Of course, we were hypocrites, since our own cell phones were filled with text messages. Generation text—average age eighteen to twenty-five—is the generation that grew up with text messages as the norm, but the term also highlights a more prominent trend—the speed at which technology and communication continue to evolve.

We were raised in the generation that communicates electronically. Texting is normal for us. When text messaging became popular during our senior year of college, we jumped onboard. The younger someone was when she embraced texting and social media, the more ingrained it is in her communication style and life in general. But as our business grows, so does our awareness of the place for electronic communication and of where it can be misplaced in a traditional business. We had to bridge the gap between our young team members, who are used to communicating electronically, and our older team members, who aren't, and also identify what is appropriate use of social media and what is not.

The students and young people we hired are engrossed in the current culture of text messaging and social networking. As a result, it's become an integral part of our management and communication strategies. Most older employers aren't as savvy about using technology, so the younger generation needs patience with them, and the older generation needs to adapt and learn ASAP. It's important to embrace electronic media, since they're spreading fast and can help your business in many ways. But they can also cause problems if there are no systems in place to regulate them. Getting a phone call from a team member who couldn't come to work seemed like common sense and being responsible. But younger team members saw it differently. That led us to implement policies and procedures spelling out when phone calls are required and texts aren't appropriate.

We recognize and embrace technology as a rapidly changing beast. It's crucial to stay abreast of trends and how they'll affect your business and staff. If you don't evolve along with them, you'll quickly become extinct. The youthful generation is usually first to adopt and master new technology. Young people are also usually front-line team members. The majority of them have replaced e-mail with text messages and/or social networking. We've embraced their modes of communication but also recognized potential pitfalls as technology evolves. We've had to put training and systems in place to make sure new technology works well in our company.

Be careful to assess carefully what you use, so time isn't wasted using new technology that doesn't benefit your business. You should adopt a new technology only if you have a clear use and need for it, not just because it's what everyone else is doing. For example, Twitter (twitter.com/collegehunks) is useful for us, since we've built a fun, quirky, personal brand that people might want to stay connected to in a personal way and also allows us to see and respond when people talk about us. For a company like McDonald's, it may not initially make sense to use Twitter. People who eat there regularly probably aren't interested in quick snippets of what the folks at McDonald's think or in establishing a personal relationship with them. But, in fact, it's another tool for establishing a cult following for a brand even for a company as large and established as McDonald's. When thinking about technology, consider all the same questions you'd consider for any other new asset:

- What will this cost in terms of both time and financing?
- What value will this add?
- Who will be responsible for maintaining it?

Just because a technology is new and trendy, there's no reason to use it if it doesn't make sense for your business. Sure, things like Web sites and e-mail are no-brainers these days. But a company wiki or a social networking site is the sort of thing that could be very helpful for some companies and totally useless or premature for others. You have to evaluate what you use based on your client base and what benefits each technology will bring to your business. Just because someone says you should use one isn't a good reason to do it. Think hard before joining the flavor of the week in technology. Each one you use means someone needs to be paid to maintain it and procedures must be created to make the most of it.

BALANCING COMMUNICATION

While we embrace new technology, we understand that traditional communication still has an important role to play in running our business. Businesses still fax and use landline phones. Finding a balance lies in knowing when to use what type of communication and recognizing that direct face-to-face human interaction is the most powerful form of communication for achieving results. It should never be replaced. For quick, insignificant communication, a text message makes sense. E-mails, social networking messages, and tweets work too. But speaking on the phone or, more important, face-to-face is a dying form of communication that must be taught to younger people through training and role-playing.

*Create effective systems to keep your business on track
and enable individuals to succeed.*

We've spent a lot of time and money to make our software integrate alternative methods of communication. Our online scheduling system sends e-mails and text messages with the week's schedule to team members. They can log in to request time off. Our software sends auto-texts with the location of same-day jobs to the truck team. Sending a mass text message to multiple recipients at one time communicates with a group to make an announcement as opposed to contacting each person individually. We can get a point across much faster that way and we can be confident that everyone received the text message. However, we did implement a requirement that team members acknowledge all texts they receive to confirm that they actually got the message and are acting accordingly.

We send many text messages to each other daily. It helps us get things off our chests, make a quick point, or express an idea. We also have text arguments with each other to help us vent without biting the other's head off. It keeps a barrier between us and still gets our points across. As we said in chapter 5, arguments help us express feelings and get back to business. People say things in text messages that they might not say in person. We don't worry about that. We can say anything. Here's a sample text message conversation from our early days. Things haven't changed much.

Omar: *Why the f@$# did you schedule a carpet-removal job when you knew there was a pool table in the middle of the room???*

Nick: *They can fu@$#@ cut around it and lift the pool table up.*

Omar: *No they can't! They've been there for 2 damn hours. We're losing money and the team members are pissed!*

Nick: *Dude! Shut the f#@ up. I'm going to punch you in the head! They can charge labor!!*

Omar: *You moron! No they can't, it's too late. This is why our team members get so damn pissed.*

This kind of texting is just another part of going into business with your best friend. Being able to express these kinds of feelings is helpful, as long as you're willing and able to take as much as you dish out. Texting can be used as a shield. Like e-mail, it's a good way to communicate without feeling, to avoid an uncomfortable face-to-face conversation or interaction. It's easier to type a message and hit Send than to pick up the phone and deal with emotions, or, even more difficult, sit down with the person. People don't like uncomfortable situations, and dealing with people can be uncomfortable.

Team members who feel uneasy asking questions or speaking up verbally may text what they want. For example, we had a staff meeting to address team members' concerns and opened it up for comments and questions. No one spoke when given the opportunity. But the day after, Nick got a text message from one person: *I wanted to ask at the meeting about health benefits. I've been payin my own for a while and would love to get somethin started thru the company. Need to save loot for school comin up.*

The younger generation prefers raising issues and concerns by text messaging. But in order to address major decisions in our company, we insist on face-to-face meetings.

People prefer to hide behind a computer or text. This can backfire if messages are misinterpreted. Exclamation points in a text message can make it seem like you're yelling. Text communications with clients are rare unless they initiate them. Because more personal communication is important, we instituted Telephone Tuesdays and Thank-You Thursdays, since nowadays it's rare for a client to receive a phone call from someone he does business with. We call five clients every Tuesday. It's even more rare to receive a handwritten note, so we write five thank-you notes every Thursday. You'll be a lot more successful if you embrace human interaction. We also instituted Walk-In Wednesdays, when we just show up at a client's business to say hello.

BRINGING OLDER TEAM MEMBERS AND FRANCHISEES UP TO TEXT

We introduced text messages to our older vendors, colleagues, and franchisees to communicate with one another and with us. Once our thirty-plus-year-old team members and franchisees began texting, it was much faster and more effective than phone calls or e-mails. We have a few corporate team members and franchisees who are over fifty and weren't raised with this technology. Something had to be done when we started expanding and recognized a potential generation gap that could hold us back.

Our director of franchise development had never sent a text message or conducted a virtual conference. Our comprehensive software was overwhelming for him. We needed a way to bring everyone at least close to the same digital level, but there wasn't time or resources to fully train someone on every aspect of the new technology. So we added a two-hour crash course on the basics of text messaging, virtual conferencing, e-mail organizing and calendars, Facebook, Skype, Web conferencing, and other neat resources that can be taken advantage of online. We called this "Back to the Future Training" and opened it to anyone in the company on a monthly basis.

Now our director of franchise development uses virtual conferences to speak with prospective franchisees. He text messages more than anyone in the company and even has his own Facebook and LinkedIn pages, where he networks with other franchise-development colleagues across the country. His communications with everyone in the organization and his time are now maximized. The result? More franchise sales! We've cut costs with virtual training and support, since our staff needs less travel. Text messaging is very efficient because team members and franchisees aren't in front of computers all day.

The call center reps text message job notes and reminders. We can sync people's calendars with their e-mail so everyone is on the same page for upcoming conferences, to-do lists, and meetings. Older team members and franchisees flourished the most. They have more wisdom and business experience but were hindered by technology. Now they can add even more value. Some cool online resources are:

- Dimdim.com has resources for free Web conferencing.
- GoToMeeting.com and ReadyTalk.com provide Web conferencing for a fee.
- Jing.com has domain hosting and e-mail services, and allows you to create free online training videos.
- FreeConferenceCall.com does exactly what its name states.
- Yammer.com allows you to create a message board forum that can be saved and categorized.
- BrainKeeper.com allows you to create an internal company wiki like Wikipedia.
- Ning.com allows you to create your own internal company social network.
- ManyMoon.com allows you to track and manage multiple projects at once.

BRINGING BACK CLIENT SERVICE

It became imperative to bridge the technology gap between younger team members and older clients. One of our service standards is to call clients twenty minutes before their appointment window. Younger team members weren't comfortable speaking on the phone. We took for granted that they knew how to be cordial and polite, but the average eighteen- to twenty-five-year-old doesn't talk much to older people by phone and found it extremely uncomfortable. So getting them to make a courtesy phone call on the way actually involved a steep learning curve, for them and us. We had to set up a training system.

The text message generation has lost personal interaction skills required of a front-line team member. These days, adolescents break up with their significant other via text message. There's a psychological and technological gap between the front-line generation text and older, less tech-savvy consumers. As a result, what used to be commonsense client service must be thoroughly taught in training sessions to eighteen- to twenty-five-year-old team members. Everything is electronic these days—banking, shopping, socializing.

Many Gen Texts lack human-interaction skills. We've had to teach and encourage the lost art of client service and the human-interaction experience that older generations crave. We trained team members in how to speak with clients over the phone. We developed a training program that includes interactive skills—team members role-play the client interaction in order to help emphasize those people skills needed by front-line employees that may have been lost over the years as a result of new technology.

Develop staff, client, and community loyalty.

We have a large generation gap between team members and clients, many of whom are baby boomers or a few years younger. Our training paints a picture of the type of service our clients expect and wish for. The older generation often complains about lack of service in places that used to offer amazing service. They remember when they shopped in local independent stores instead of the larger chains. People were on a first-name basis. So we combine the efficiency of technology with the personalization of old-school service. Team members understand this, since we make it clear that when they walk into a home, they're not video-game-playing know-it-all kids. They are a reflection of our clients when they were younger and hardworking. Team members can't go out in the field until they understand that we're selling an experience just as much as a service. We teach the basics:

- How to shake someone's hand
- The importance of making eye contact
- To say "yes" instead of "yeah"
- How to speak confidently and not mumble
- Proper posture
- How to wear the uniform
- To always say "please," "thank you," and "my pleasure"

This seems like Manners 101 but for many in this generation it's more like teaching advanced math. But it pays off when clients are floored by the quality of our service. We get many e-mails and calls saying how "polite and courteous" our teams are. Some people feel such an emotional connection to the level of service we provide that they want to help our company succeed however they can. Clients request specific team members each time they use us—even two years later. The team members bristled in the beginning, but we ingrained this courteousness into the culture and training. When new team members see how veterans act, they try their best to imitate what they see. In the long run it keeps everyone—clients, team members, and us—happy.

BRANDING ONLINE

We recently hired a PR intern from a local college to help with our online presence and branding. The result? A 50 percent improvement in our search engine optimization as well as increased team member participation in company social groups. Using online tools offers unlimited potential for branding your business online. If you can get some tech-savvy interns to help you, it can be an inexpensive investment in your future. Right now about 30 percent of business comes from our Web site.

Image is everything.

Start-up businesses usually create a Web site right away. If you hire a designer, a lot depends on that person's Web design skills. It can be difficult to communicate to the Web designer what kind of layout you want and the look you envision. A Web site's home page is like a storefront. It needs to beckon people to come in and make them feel comfortable with your product or service. The impression it creates can make or break a deal, so it's a critical building block in business. Our Web site gets rave reviews from clients and prospective franchisees and won an American Marketing Award.

It's important to identify your target clients BEFORE you design a Web site. Many of our clients are over forty. We wanted to create a site that was simple, user friendly, but sleek. If you target an older demographic, stay away from flash animation, complex designs, and Web site intros. These clients may not be as tech savvy or have an up-to-date computer. But if you target a younger demographic, consider a site that really stands out from the pack, with cool animation and more complex designs. Keep it simple, fluid, and interactive. Conceptualize the look of each page on paper. You don't need to be an artist. Just make as many notes as possible so the designer can understand how to create the site. Typical headers for your page are:

- PRICING
- SERVICES/PRODUCTS
- ABOUT US
- CONTACT/ORDER FORM

Make it easy to purchase your products or services on the spot. "Book Online" or "Order Online" forms should be very visible and accessible. It's important to capture information from anyone who visits your site. Find ways for people to leave their e-mail address, along with their city and state and other helpful info. We advise against having excessive pages and links. Make it simple for people to get pertinent information in a concise way, without having to go from page to page. You can lose people that way.

You MUST have a "Contact Us" section. People have more confidence in a company they can reach. Include a phone number, if possible. To avoid sending clients to voice mail if you or a staff member can't answer calls, consider using an answering service so a live person answers with your company name and introduction. There are inexpensive ones out there if you look.

It should be obvious on the home page what your product or service is. Many Web sites are cluttered or have too much text. The more concise your text and the fewer things to look at, the more likely people will read and want to learn more. Get your Web site noticed by buying pay-per-click ads and improving search engine optimization by making sure it's rich in keywords. If Internet marketing seems overwhelming, consider hiring an online marketing company like Yodel.com to manage your pay-per-click advertising campaigns for you.

It's imperative to have an e-mail address on your business card. DO NOT use a Gmail, AOL, or Yahoo! address on your business card. That screams bush-league! Getting your own domain is inexpensive and usually comes with a free e-mail address so even before your Web site is created, you can have a professional e-mail address on your business card. If you're just getting started and have a tight budget, you can find inexpensive designers from overseas at Odesk.com or Elance.com. Make sure you get ownership of the code so you can replace your initial Web designers down the road.

USING SOCIAL NETWORKING SITES

Picture your clients and potential clients as valuable marbles spread all over. Every time you need your marbles you scramble around searching for them. It's a lot better if you keep them all in a bag so that anywhere you go, they're easy to access. The digital age allows businesses to do that. The founder of the online shoe store Zappos.com has over one million people following him on Twitter. How easy do you think it is for him to announce a new shoe special coming up? Every time he types something, over a million people see it. It's 100 percent FREE to do this! How about rapper Soulja Boy, who also has a million-plus followers? He can type one sentence—"Buy my new single on iTunes!"—and his faithful followers all click and download the single.

Twitter, Facebook, and blogging are all tactics that allow you to keep clients informed, attentive, and organized. There's no magic wand. These social media platforms take work to develop and skill to take advantage of effectively. Each one can be tied to the other. Our three main objectives with social media are to:

- Be viewed as the experts in our industry
- Communicate the cool/fun factor of working at College Hunks Hauling Junk
- Allow the general public to become friends with the founders and vice versa

Notice that our objectives do *not* mention increasing sales or acquiring more clients. Those are by-products of a successful online branding campaign, not our focus. We want the public to know that College Hunks Hauling Junk is the expert in the junk-hauling business and anyone in the world can become part of our company culture. Getting people to discuss us online creates a cool factor about working at our company.

Develop staff, client, and community loyalty.

New technology helps us build team spirit. We text congratulations for college graduations and birthdays and post media hits to each franchise's Web page. As a fresh new company, College Hunks Hauling Junk had its own Facebook page early on. Now most companies have one. We also created a private company site just for team members to interact. Members can post pictures of themselves and message one another, helping us build the cohesive national team we envisioned. Our company has become a cool place to work and we're inundated with résumés.

We use Facebook as much as possible to maintain relationships with our team members, clients, and friends. The College Hunks Hauling Junk group and fan page has hundreds of current and past team members. The page is filled with pictures, team member updates, and discussions. When you click on the page, it's hard not to feel the company culture emanating from the screen. Anybody can join the group and go from being a spectator to a friend to participating in discussions. This has been a great tool for recruitment. Friends of team members see the fun atmosphere and want to join. We also have all our media and funny YouTube videos as well as video testimonials linked on the site. Prospective employees and franchisees can see what a unique experience it is to work for us or become a franchise owner.

Many of our franchisees created Facebook pages, and we had to reel them in to make sure they didn't compromise the brand image. If one of our employees or franchisees has personal information on Facebook and it shows him or her partying or doing something inappropriate, it can reflect negatively on the brand. One of our franchisees posted a YouTube video of our company mascot dancing inappropriately. These are just examples of the online media realities of today that businesses have to face. There is much less room to hide and much more access to the people and personalities behind an organization. A policy must be developed and included in your company handbook.

Our blogs focus more on professional tips, links, and updates about maintaining a clutter-free home. We inform the public about where to take hazardous materials, share videos about proper garage-organizing techniques, and more. We blog as experts in our industry. The key to blogging and all social media is to UPDATE, UPDATE, and UPDATE. The more times a week, day, or hour you update your blogs, Facebook, and Twitter with relevant information, the more people want to tune in. There's nothing worse than a blog that hasn't been updated in weeks. It feels like walking into a ghost town. You can also hurt your efforts by sending updates that seem like spam. You want people to check your blog consistently to see what new information or updates were added.

Twitter gives the public a chance to follow our executives. Our tweets aren't just about the business. We share with everyone what we're doing, what city we're in, or a funny occurrence. People don't want to follow someone who's constantly pushing his business or an advertisement down their throat. Instead, they want insight into what your daily life is like. We do try to share helpful tips about running a business and what's going on at College Hunks Hauling Junk, but we also tell you when we're a bit hungover after a night of partying.

All social networks are connected. Our tweets sometimes direct people to our blog, our blog posts direct people to our Facebook page, and so on. The more informative your blog posts, the more people will share your links. Giving solid information makes others want to share it. If bloggers and tweeters like what you write, they'll point their followers to your Web site, blog, or Twitter. The more inbound links your blog and Web site can acquire, the better search results you'll get in Google and Yahoo! searches. As a result, our pool of followers has grown, our pool of team members has grown, and our Web site visits have grown.

As founders, we strive to be just one degree of separation away from anybody anywhere. Got a question, comment, or cheap shot? We'll respond to just about anything. The days of CEOs hiding behind big mahogany desks with a gatekeeper secretary are over. Today we strive to be just as accessible as our front-line team members. We also send daily words of wisdom tweets to anybody who subscribes via Twitter. Find us at:

Nick: twitter.com/NickFriedman1
Omar: twitter.com/omarjunkman
www.facebook.com/collegehunks
http://www.linkedin.com/in/collegehunkshaulingjunk
www.1800Junkusa.com/blog

CHAPTER 10

DEATH OF THE SALESMAN
Optimizing Your Ability to Make the Sale

Nick got an invitation—a time-share pitch—to tour a hotel and receive a free three-night stay. He attended the presentation and tour with zero intention of buying anything and every intention of enjoying the three-night stay. Everything was perfectly scripted. The salespeople made their time-share packages sound spectacular and one-of-a-kind. Everyone was assigned a salesperson. If you said no, he brought in a sales manager. Several people bought a package, which wasn't cheap. Nick had to slap himself when he started to seriously consider it. The salespeople tried every coercive, mind-controlling tactic to convince Nick to buy. He didn't, but learned how *not* to make a sales pitch. Salespeople get a bad name because of these kinds of manipulative tactics, yet such tactics are extremely effective. Nick left determined to find a better way. He brainstormed with Omar for strategies.

UNDERSTANDING SALES

Our parents gave sales a bad rap when we were growing up, so we viewed it negatively. *Salespeople* evoked an image of someone pushing used cars or selling snake oil door-to-door. Nick's mom scoffed at his interest in sales, though his personality was suited to it. But the truth is, to succeed in any area of life, it's vital to understand how to sell to, connect with, and relate to people, whether you sell a product, a service, or yourself. Everything you go after relates to sales—in business and life. You sell yourself at a job interview, to your future spouse, and any time you want something.

Even if you don't actively sell in the purest sense, you're selling. In the corporate world, your résumé determines if you get a face-to-face meeting. A job interview is an opportunity to sell yourself to an employer. If you meet someone at a bar, you sell yourself as worthy of a date. On a date, you sell yourself as an ideal mate or as someone to go home with. While sales may be perceived negatively, learning how to sell is one of the best life skills you can develop to succeed at almost anything you embark on, especially business. You sell concepts and, most important, yourself and your vision when pitching potential investors to raise capital.

When done properly, selling can be not only the most profitable profession, but also a noble one. After all, if you have a great product or service that you sincerely believe clients can benefit from, then doing your best to get them to try it is not only profitable, but the right thing to do. The image of the sleazy used-car salesman exists only because those people need to use tricks to sell products without real value. If you have a company with integrity and a product you believe in, then it's easy to be an effective salesperson while maintaining your integrity. It's important to follow a system for selling that others can follow. When you hire salespeople, make sure they have a proven sales track record and are motivated by money and willing to be compensated on the basis of performance.

Create effective systems to keep your business on track and enable individuals to succeed.

Following a solid system helps it become second nature. We figured out effective sales techniques the hard way. After realizing that creating a good sales system was crucial to our success, we were concerned that we had no real-world experience, until we recognized that everything we'd attempted to gain—popularity, girls, grades, and jobs—required sales. Generating attention in school, assuming leadership, talking ourselves out of trouble all took strong sales skills. Effective sales requires:

- Having a target or target pool
- Knowing how to pitch them
- Picking up the phone and calling them
- Following up if you don't hear back

You should be able to illustrate the value of your product or service by communicating why your target client should buy from you. The ability to sell hinges on relationship building. People buy from and do business with people they like. Connect on a personal level first and then sell. It's important to distinguish sales from deceit. The time-share salespeople were manipulative and gave a high-pressure pitch. Sometimes those types can be misleading or try to scare you into buying. Inspirational styles of sales create the most potential for long-term loyalty if you deliver on your promises, which we do.

Image is everything.

We want to do business with people who believe what we believe so that there's an authenticity about what we do. It's much more effective for creating a brand that lasts. You're no longer selling, you're helping. The idea that inspired your business in the first place must be carried out. Without execution, it's all hot air. Our goal as a company has been to inspire people to buy from us based on our entrepreneurial spirit, energy, and collegiate company culture. Those three simple inspirational tools were more effective in gaining a loyal client base than telling them we help them get rid of junk. Our line "Let Tomorrow's Leaders Haul Your Junk Today" is an inspirational message about youth working hard for their future. It's also an authentic sales pitch that attracts and keeps our customers coming back and recommending us to new ones.

RAPPORT + TRUST = COMFORT

A big hurdle in sales is maintaining confidence. It's hard, and downright demoralizing, to continue pursuing a sale after hearing the hundred *no*s that can come before that one *yes*. That's why it's so difficult to hire people without sales experience. They need too much time to get over their fear of hearing *no*. Accepting that every *no* is just a stepping-stone and each and every one must be stepped on to succeed makes it easier to tolerate them and keep going. Potential clients will be more comfortable and more likely to do business with you if you create a good rapport and earn their trust.

Making sure you have an attractive image will get you noticed—in dating and in business. But once you've attracted someone, you need to sell her on you or your company. Just as your appearance can make you stand out in an attractive way to get someone's attention in a club, having an appealing brand helps you get your foot in the door. But when the conversation starts, you still have to close the deal. Even a perfect image won't help if you don't know how to make the sale. It takes both branding and sales to get clients, just as you should try to both look good and be a good communicator if you want to leave the club with phone numbers. Those same factors help you get appointments with potential clients and make the sale.

We honed our sales confidence in bars with our friend Brett, who fancied himself a pickup artist. There's nothing more demoralizing to a young male than to get rejected repeatedly when speaking to girls. Brett says the more girls you approach, the greater the likelihood that one will like what you say and be interested. As in sales, your technique should be refined each time to adjust and improve. Brett made a game of it.

Like warming up with an assortment of shots before playing basketball, Brett practiced with less attractive girls and easy girls to build confidence. Then he'd talk to better-looking ones. As in a basketball game, if his shot was off he'd go back to layups, so he'd score either way. While we didn't buy into this method of meeting girls, Brett encouraged us to practice his techniques. Not only did we get better and more confident at talking with girls, but our sales skills improved and nothing could stop us from attempting to make the sale. Attempting is the most important part. You miss 100 percent of the sales pitches you don't make.

Whether you're a girl or a guy, how many times do you see someone attractive at a bar or coffee shop but not have the guts to start a conversation? If you make it a game, the pursuit, drive, and achievement are the best parts. Brett encouraged us to strike up conversations with girls. Doing so made us more immune to the word *no*. It just rolled off our backs. Just as the best basketball players don't remember the last shot they missed, good salespeople never remember the big account they lost, and pickup artists never remember those who rejected them. After learning how to meet girls, we had no qualms about making cold calls, stopping into offices to ask for the manager, or asking for referrals.

Work ON the business from the outside, not IN it.

Some days the phone seemed heavier and checking e-mail seemed easier than making sales stops, attending networking functions, following up with prospects, or making cold calls. Then we'd remember Brett. If he put half as much effort into making sales calls as he did into trying to sell himself to girls, he'd be a millionaire ten times over! Eventually our sales techniques were systemized so that others could sell while we worked ON the business. We joke with Brett that he should systemize his pickup style so others could make phone calls to girls for him. After watching him, the more girls we spoke to, the more numbers we got. Our close percentage improved. We practiced and honed our pitch by focusing on important factors that enhance a successful sales process:

- *Express a time constraint:* Put a deal on the table that won't be good indefinitely. When people have a deadline or know the offer is limited, they respond more quickly.
- *Have a script:* Plan what you'll say to people you want to sell to. Don't try to wing it. The more you use the pitch, the better you'll become at selling your product or service. It becomes more of an art. Manipulative salespeople have a response or retort for every objection. Inspirational salespeople look for a personal connection and build on it. It's important to spark an interest with your opener, but LISTEN first.
- *Exhibit social proof:* People want what they believe others want and do what others do. So if others use your company or it was written about in the local newspaper, that establishes social proof that it must be worth using.
- *Establish value:* If a carpet cleaner walked into your home and quoted you a price of $500 to clean your carpets, you might have no idea whether that was fair. But if before mentioning price he explained everything he'd do, what type of shampoo he'd use, how long the carpet would stay clean, and how safe his cleaning products were, he would establish the value of his services, and you would know what you're paying for.

- *Identify scarcity:* Scarcity is the idea that people want something that's limited in supply. Even if our schedule is wide open, we suggest it may be a busy week, which encourages people to schedule their appointment.
- *Ask for the close:* The close is essentially asking for the sale or an appointment. Use assumptive closes like "When can we meet?" instead of "Can we meet?" or an alternative close like "Shall we meet on Friday or Saturday?" If you don't ask for the close, you leave yourself in limbo. You typically get only one chance to ask, so don't blow your opportunity by asking at the wrong time. If you walk up to someone and ask for his or her number, you'll most likely get shot down. If you call your ideal client and ask for a sale without the previous steps in the process, you may blow any opportunity to do business with that person.
- *Suggest steps the person can take next:* Once you've established the close, you're now the authority and must dictate the next steps. If it's a sales meeting, suggest a time. If the time needs to be changed later on, so be it.

This worked to Nick's advantage one night at a Miami nightclub. As we tried to get in, four beautiful girls—clear-cut 10s—approached. One caught Nick's eye as they were whisked through the velvet rope. Omar talked our way in, as always. As we waited for drinks at the bar, the girls walked by. Nick tried to get the attention of the one who'd caught his eye by taking her hand. She shot him a look and walked away. Later, she returned to the bar. Nick went for a second try, even thought she'd rebuffed him. He confidently asked, "Didn't you see me trying to stop you earlier?" "No, I was with my friends," she said. They made small talk.

Nick mentioned that he was in town for only a few days (*time constraint*), that we were staying at a condo on the beach (*value*), that he wanted to take her to a restaurant his friend worked at (*social proof*), and that he didn't have many nights free (*scarcity*). Nick told her to give him her number so he could call her about the dinner, and she gave it to him (*close*). In life, as in business, you need to be confident and not accept the first *no* as final. Wait a while and try again. But after two or three *no*s, move on to the next would-be client or date. In dating, the goal is to get a number for a future meeting. In business, you want an appointment that gets the SALE. Use the same skills in a social setting that you use in business, and vice versa, to improve both. The best relationships in business and social situations are long term, with purpose and meaning. One-night stands and one-off clients are fool's gold.

As our confidence improved, so did the attractiveness of the girls we felt comfortable approaching. With girls, there are 10s, 9s, etc. In business, there are A, B, and C clients. The C clients are easy to get but much less desirable. They're price picky and don't value you. B clients are a little better. A clients are the dream ones. They value what you provide, are happy to pay your rate, and look for ways to refer new business to you.

When you start your business, you'll likely take all clients, but your focus should be on A clients. Settling for second- or third-rate ones will demean your position as a service or product provider. If you close a sale in the first meeting, it's a B or a C client. The C client that uses you to fulfill an immediate need and isn't interested in setting up a long-term business relationship is like someone who sleeps with you the first night and never calls you again.

BUILDING RELATIONSHIPS

Selling for the long term isn't like selling widgets door-to-door. A key to long-term sales success is seeing potential clients as being good for a lot more than one sale. One-off sales don't grow a business. The relationships you develop at the outset will. Try to define your core client. What can you offer that's unique? How can you inspire him to buy from you without driving yourself crazy trying to compete with other companies?

Develop staff, client, and community loyalty.

Repeat and referral business is your bread and butter. When you establish relationships, instead of forcing just one sale and moving on, your business grows. Eighty percent of our business comes from 20 percent of our clients. It's important to recognize this for two reasons. One, you must always stay fresh for that 20 percent core as you wade through the 80 percent. Two, while you strive for success, you can't always bend over backwards for every single client. Keep in mind that the quality 20 percent are waiting for you. We've identified strategies that have substantially helped us build relationships with potential clients and those we've worked with:

- *Commitment and consistency.* Be consistent with clients and get a commitment when you can.
- *Likability.* Get clients to like you by looking for connection points between you and playing those points up. Key elements include physical appearance, compliments, similarities, and familiarity.
- *Authority.* Be an authority figure. When a client feels he's dealing with an authority figure based on your title, appearance, and attitude, he's more likely to say *yes.*
- *Community standing.* Good community relations and testimonials go a long way in building credibility. Giving back to your community in some way will improve your image with clients.
- *Reciprocation.* Try to repay in kind what another person does for you. Early on we joined a great small-business networking association called Business Network International (BNI). Its philosophy is "Givers Gain." If you pass out referrals for other members of the group, you get rewarded by getting referrals from them. People typically try to return favors with much more than they got.

Even when there's no sale, save people's information. You might get them later. If you write them off and toss their info, you'll have to gather it again if they return or you follow up and try to rekindle their interest. For example, Nick met an executive from a large company at a networking function and followed up afterwards to set up a partnership with College Hunks Hauling Junk. Nick proposed an alliance to become their outsourced hauler. The VP was interested, but corporate politics initially got in the way. Nick kept in touch. After two years of periodic contact, a deal was struck.

Sales is like a funnel. If you don't keep putting things in the top of the funnel, eventually things will stop coming out the bottom. And if you don't have someone at the bottom to catch the sales and foster a long-term relationship, eventually clients will go to a competitor. The goal in business is to shorten the sales cycle as much as possible and go from initial contact to sale as quickly as possible. Some deals take longer to materialize. Often the best ones take time.

Don't lose the ability to enlarge the sales funnel based on the information you gather. You must have a way to report the funnel. Make a list of prospects who are considering a quote or ready to make a decision and a list of your active accounts that are being pursued. You must find a way (mail merge, e-mail blast) to regularly put your name in front of the target market based on the info collected. Constant Contact, Jango Mail, and iContact are e-mail marketing firms that offer tools to help you to maintain communication with clients and prospects.

"DATING" A PROSPECTIVE CUSTOMER

Some lines work well in romance. Likewise, "patter"—effective quips and phrases—should always be on the tip of your tongue when you're talking to a prospective customer. Pat phrases and pitches are also advantageous for most aspects of doing business. They help fill gaps in conversation and give a bit of levity to a sales pitch so that there's never a lull. Patter in a social environment includes catchy openers that aren't cheesy. At College Hunks Hauling Junk, we have fun patter that includes:

- Junk today, GONE today.
- Use us once and you'll put us on speed dial.
- I was a College Hunk, but I graduated, so now I'm just a hunk!

Create your own patter with phrases that apply to your business. Learn and practice using them to sound natural. Patter should never replace meaningful conversation, but it's useful filler. It can be an opener if you're uncomfortable and is helpful if you're nervous about making your first sales pitches. Having one-liners that add humor and get a point across creates a connection with people. They may remember a clever catchphrase or a funny line and associate it with you. The more you use patter, the more natural and automatic it becomes. That builds confidence, since it keeps the dialogue flowing.

It's also imperative to know all facets of what you're selling—inside and out. Have a specific story of a client you've helped to share. When Omar had a day job in sales, he was assigned to call prospective target clients and set up appointments for his sales director. He was responsible for making a prospect interested enough to be willing to meet with the salesperson above him, who asked for the sale. But Omar had zero idea what his company did or the products it sold. During the weekly sales roundups, Omar's numbers reflected that. He tried to learn but his head was swimming when he read the materials and binders of information. It was all too boring. Like patter, the details about your products or services should always be right on the tip of your tongue.

When you have great lines and answers, put them to good use. Any time you go out, whether to a bar or to a business networking event, you never know whom you'll meet. Being out and about provides opportunities to talk up your business, share a story about a client you helped, and make contacts to optimize your chances for business success. We shared our story and vision with anyone willing to listen. Everyone is a potential customer. We were unfazed by people who were indifferent or negative and simply moved on to find people willing to listen.

In dating, you don't want to appear desperate or chase someone too hard. It's the same with potential clients. If you have a hot sales prospect who doesn't return your call, you have to cut bait. Leave a message or e-mail saying, "XYZ, when we met you expressed an interest in meeting again to learn more about our services. Since then, I left you a message but haven't heard from you. I'll assume you no longer need our services. If I'm mistaken, let me know. Otherwise, I wish you nothing but the best." Be friendly, polite, and professional. In business or pleasure, people are more attracted to those who don't seem to need them.

Leaving a message that stops your efforts to make the sale helps you avoid obsessing over lingering prospects. That gives you more time and energy to move to the next fish, because there are ALWAYS more fish. If you get stuck trying to catch a specific one, you may be better off moving to a new fishing hole. People tend to get tunnel vision and think that one person is the be-all and end-all of their livelihood. No one is that important! You're much better off cutting communication. Your message might entice a call from the person later on. We've learned to teach our franchisees how to fish—we don't do all the sales work for them. That's part of our sales system. And, what do you do when the fish stop biting? You learn to hunt.

Convincing someone to go with your product or service involves building her trust in your ability and the quality of your product. The elements of your communication can make or break a sale, no matter how good the service or product is. Train yourself to think and speak directly to the prospect and her needs. Don't generalize too much. Use *you* as much as possible. "Why is this important to you?" "Our product/service will help you by _____." This approach keeps it personal so the prospect connects more. Create a level of comfort in your dialogue. Don't talk *at* her. Talk *with* her. Make your pitch seem more like a conversation than a push to do business with you.

Your attitude is an important factor in determining success. Develop a positive, productive one and put it to work for you. People respond best to a friendly, happy demeanor. A smile can be "heard" over the phone and makes you sound positive. Try to speak very clearly and slowly. This was a big lesson for us. We'd call and say, "This is Nick from College Hunks Hauling Junk." It sounded more like "This is Nick from colgeunksaulingjunk." People had no idea what we'd said. The whole benefit of the name had no effect on them. We really had to enunciate to a point where Omar made fun of Nick for how slowly he said our company name over the phone.

Make sure you listen carefully to your clients so you hear opportunities and can also come up with things to ask based on what they say. That creates a good connection. Making the sale builds your business. Finding people who are interested but don't want to close doesn't. Work on your people skills. The more you connect with potential clients, the greater your chance of getting the sale. Then follow up with an amazing experience, and sales will build as loyal clients spread the word.

SALES VS. NETWORKING OPPORTUNITIES

Make sure you have a professional business card. Attend networking events and meet as many people as possible while collecting business cards from people you think would be good referral partners or potential clients. Initially we went to lead-sharing groups and got involved with the chamber of commerce. This introduced us to other professionals who didn't have a direct opportunity to do business with us, but directed us to other networking groups and associations with our target commercial clients.

Follow up by e-mail and/or a handwritten note with everyone you think might turn into a client or a source for referrals. A generic "nice to meet you" won't cut it. We send a personal message that follows up on a particular conversation we had with the person and asks for or offers something useful. We explain what we can do, list the benefits of each service, then close with a testimonial or a link to a news story about our firm, and include a way to keep in touch. Sometimes we suggest a next step. A few people respond. Out of those, one or two are candidates for junk removal or have a referral for us.

Networking becomes a game, with a clear objective and a measurable score at the end—an eventual sale. It isn't always about looking for direct customers. Our goal in networking is to inspire and demonstrate our value to potential clients and influencers, which leads to sales if we make a connection and follow up. People like to talk about themselves, so at networking events ask the people you meet about themselves first and foremost. "What brings you here?" Or turn the conversation to their story if they ask you questions. "And how about you?" This creates a personal connection that can lead to more people who might use your product or services.

CHAPTER 11

SYSTEMIZING YOUR BUSINESS

FOR THE LONG HAUL
Using a Franchise Model
Even If You Don't Franchise

We were anxious to grow into the national brand we promoted. College Hunks Hauling Junk had the facade of a national company, operated like a national company, and led people to believe that we *were* a national company. We knew it was time to start to grow into our image. We were doing well, but didn't have the capital to invest in many cities at once, nor did we want to make that kind of financial investment. After brainstorming like crazy, franchising our company seemed like the best fit for our long-term goals. We wanted to own junk removal and have our brand known across the country. Franchising looked like the fastest way to accomplish that. In school we organized our peers to follow us into mischief and other activities. So why not find others with an entrepreneurial spirit who might want to follow our business model?

We felt ready to work with people who wanted their own business but didn't have the funds, desire, or knowledge to start from scratch. If we came up with the right terms, we could get these kindred entrepreneurs onboard to buy a College Hunks Hauling

Junk franchise. With the same attitude we used to get people to follow us onto a football field or to crash parties, we decided to motivate others to join our company. By having independent franchise owners implement our systems and pay us a percentage of their sales, we could grow a residual stream of income for ourselves, and eventually we'd have even more time to pursue other ventures because of it. Deciding to become a franchised business was our biggest step toward growing into a national company.

Following a franchise model is an essential step for every business owner, whether you plan to franchise your business or not. The best way for any entrepreneur—and we do mean any—to make the final jump from working IN the business to working ON it is to organize it and set up systems as if you plan to franchise it. This doesn't mean you actually will. Franchising is great for some businesses but doesn't make sense for many others. Either way, going through the process of making it franchisable is the best way to create systems that allow you to step outside the day-to-day operations of your business and deal with issues you'd rather focus on, without affecting productivity or profitability. Having these systems in place increases the value of your business and makes you replaceable, which adds to the appeal if you choose to sell it down the road.

WHY FRANCHISE?

Many new and aspiring entrepreneurs are hungry to start a business of their own, but most don't know how to get started. They also don't have the funds or know-how to get enough financing to endure the trial-and-error learning curve associated with growing a new business from scratch. These people tend to benefit most from buying a franchise, because many more new franchises succeed than new businesses do. There's an unlimited pool of people looking for the right franchise opportunity. Someone who takes over a franchise has a support system that isn't there when he starts a new business on his own.

Franchising your business allows you to scale it out much more quickly than opening additional locations one at a time. Once you've spent time and money learning how to run your business, franchising is something to consider if you want to expand your brand faster. Many top business leaders consider franchising the most successful business model to follow. Many popular businesses you're familiar with are franchises: fast-food chains, gas companies with stations around the country, doughnut shop brands. Each is owned in a franchise arrangement. A franchisor is the person or company that grants a franchise—we are franchisors. A franchisee is one who is granted a franchise to market a company's goods or services in a specific location.

People franchise their business for three main reasons: lack of money, lack of time, or lack of resources. We lacked all three. In order to reach our vision of being a nationwide brand, we had two choices. We could fork over $100K of our own money for each city—over $2 million just to open in twenty locations, plus additional expenses to staff and manage each one. Or we could franchise, which would give us a capital infusion for each one sold, and leverage the effort and equity of the franchise partners.

We figured it all out by reading books, researching the franchise industry, and joining the International Franchise Association.

Create effective systems to keep your business on track and enable individuals to succeed.

A franchise system gives someone a piece of a business that's already credible and unique. The most important factor for a franchise is that it's systemized, which means a franchisee doesn't have to create her own systems from day one. A franchisee is in business for herself, but not by herself. She uses the systems, infrastructure, branding, and support of the parent company and the other franchise owners. Franchisees make the day-to-day decisions about their business, such as staffing, advertising, and marketing plans. We do our best to find potential franchisees who share business sensibility.

Mistakes are problems only if you do not learn from them.

Owning a franchise saves the person years of learning and making costly mistakes that could put him out of business before he gets his enterprise off the ground. Franchising has many of the advantages of having a business partner. We don't interact as often with our franchisees as we do with each other, but they know we're here if they need us. We do provide consistent, ongoing support with weekly strategy and goal setting, daily troubleshooting, monthly metrics, and quarterly strategic planning.

As we said in chapter 6, in the game of business, franchisees can start close to the level that the parent company is at. Much as with the warp zones in the old game *Super Mario Brothers*, franchisees can skip to Level 5 of the game without having to go through Levels 1–4. There will be a learning curve and the initial branding of the company in the market they start in. But they still begin quite a bit above Level 1, where other new businesses begin. We've played the game and worked our way up. Our franchisees benefit from that.

Ours is a business opportunity franchise that allows someone to own and operate his own business. There are variations on the model that you can look into if you choose to go in this direction with your business. Each franchise is like a joint venture between the franchisor and the franchisee. You can open branches of your company in other locations and hire people to run them, but that sets up more potential for problems, since you can't be everywhere to oversee them. It's also a big investment for each market.

Like a partner, someone who owns a franchise is more likely to work hard and be dedicated to its success than is someone you hire to run a branch. A franchisee has a serious vested interest in the success of your company, not just her franchise. If College Hunks Hauling Junk doesn't do well or goes under, it affects everyone. So all our franchisees support the brand as a whole, knowing the good of the whole company makes theirs better.

People purchase College Hunks Hauling Junk franchises to get a turnkey operation with detailed systems, award-winning marketing strategies, operating manuals, and the support of an executive team dedicated to the success of the franchisees. A franchise is like a comprehensive business toolbox accompanied by a detailed instruction manual. In return for the support and brand power we provide, franchisees pay a percentage of revenues (royalty). Every time we sell a franchise, our market share increases, making our brand more valuable.

Our first franchisee recognized the value of owning a franchise. Faisal Ansari was twenty-five and always wanted to own a business. He considered going back to school, but then he researched franchise opportunities. Faisal realized that getting an MBA would cost about $80,000. After going to school for two years, he'd have a great degree, an excellent education, and a big debt, but not much else. He concluded that if he invested that money in a franchise, he'd get real-world business experience that a classroom rarely teaches. And after two years he might have an asset that earned an income instead of having just a degree. He wanted to invest in himself rather than in a degree.

Faisal's dad supported his seemingly risky decision and helped him purchase a College Hunks Hauling Junk franchise in Orlando, Florida. He had so much success and fun running that operation that he bought one in Tampa too. This is a new trend. With the shift in the economy, parents increasingly recognize the potential benefits for their son or daughter of launching a business venture just out of college instead of going to business school or getting a job, which was the traditional path. We were lucky. Faisal verbally committed to buying a franchise before we even put the process in place. Knowing that we'd have one franchisee open right off the bat was a big relief.

Work ON the business, not IN it.

Selling the first franchise was a momentous occasion, like putting down the first brick of a new building. Plus, it sounded better to say that we had locations in D.C. and Orlando, for both clients and potential franchisees. We knew we were on our way. After Orlando, our initial goal was to sell five franchises, and we hit it. San Francisco, Los Angeles, Denver, Raleigh, and Tampa sold in the first eight months of our franchising venture. Now we could honestly say we were a national company! Franchises can be sold one at a time and grow exponentially.

Start with a vision, create a strategic plan, and live by it.

If our vision had not been to grow College Hunks Hauling Junk as a national brand, we'd never have chosen this path. But systemizing our business in order to franchise it strengthened our brand and our operating procedures even more, making us a more powerful beast. We didn't hesitate to lay down hundreds of thousands of dollars for customized software, or to move to Tampa to set up our call center. We were in it for the long haul, no pun intended.

FINDING THE RIGHT PEOPLE

A good franchise system establishes a positive, synergistic relationship between the franchisor and franchisees. Just because a person has the money to buy a franchise doesn't mean he's right for it. If you choose to franchise your business, also choose to align yourself only with people who buy into your company vision, agree with your basic principles, are comfortable and happy to follow your system, and want the franchise because of those factors. They operate under your brand, so it's important to find like-minded people. A franchisee who veers too far from what your company is known for can hurt your brand. There are more considerations than just finding people who want to do what you did.

It can be enticing, especially early on, to sell a franchise to everyone willing to stroke a check for the fee. That's a lot of money! But if there are red flags, heed them. Money can make you overlook crucial warning signs. We terminated negotiations for a franchise relationship just before it was too late. This particular prospect had a lot of money but took up a ton of time and energy and caused many headaches before he signed the agreement. We talked ourselves into letting him join by rationalizing that his issues were eccentricities. He pushed us over the edge when he called other franchisees and complained about us before sending his check. We finally told him NO THANKS. To this day we're grateful that we saw the light before he paid. Some of the best deals are the ones you don't make.

Not everyone works out, even if he has terrific qualities. We had a model employee we'll call Alex. He was wholeheartedly bought into the company vision. Alex wore the company shirt off the clock, arrived early, worked late, put our sign on his lawn and magnets on his car. He worked for us during a semester off from school. When he returned to finish senior year, his last words were "I'm opening a franchise when I graduate, wherever you want it. I'll be like Johnny Appleseed, planting College Hunks

Hauling Junk across the country!" He kept in touch over the year and was proud that while all his friends would be getting prestigious jobs, earning entry-level salaries, and working a hundred hours a week, he'd be building equity in a business of his own.

When Alex graduated, we worked out a sweet deal that would permit him to earn equity in his own College Hunks Hauling Junk business. He understood that we couldn't offer him large benefits or a cushy salary to start, but as an employee who would eventually earn ownership in a franchise he knew the potential in the future. Unfortunately, unlike Faisal's parents, Alex's didn't share his vision. They pictured him on the traditional path out of college, in a "secure" job with benefits and upward corporate growth potential. Alex had to abandon his dream and get a "real job." His last words to us were "I'm going to save up my own capital to buy my own operation."

As we said earlier, parents often don't support entrepreneurial goals, and once people enter the rat race it can become difficult to escape. Despite Alex's proclamation and independence, we doubt he'll ever get the support of his parents, and it could take forever to raise the necessary capital working the corporate rat race, which likely means he'll never own a franchise. Many parents want their kids to be safe and secure instead of taking risks in their professional lives, so unless they have a way to raise capital themselves, their kids never take the leap to own a business. They'll follow the secure and often grueling path of climbing a corporate ladder, often with no fulfillment or freedom. Make sure candidates are available and able to take on a business. Good intentions aren't enough. We've come up with qualities that we look for in people who are interested in owning a College Hunks Hauling Junk franchise. A candidate must be:

- *A team player:* Everyone within our company is part of our team. Someone who prefers to operate above everyone else won't fit in well here. Our company culture makes everyone important.
- *Funded properly:* While our fees aren't exorbitant, we don't want someone who has to scrape his last dollars together to pay for it. Prospective franchisees need to have at least some cash flow when they get started or good enough credit to borrow what might be needed to start up properly. They also must be able to launch the brand in their market, support themselves personally while the business ramps up, and have some backup in case it takes a while.
- *Willing to follow procedures and policies:* Our company works for a reason. Its systems have proven to be effective. If someone questions them too much—for example, wants to paint the trucks a different color—he probably won't follow them. To keep our procedures and policies consistent throughout the brand, a franchisee must be enthusiastic about following them.
- *A hard worker with integrity and serious commitment:* This is a no-brainer. While we provide a system to work in, running a franchise takes as much effort as starting a business from scratch. It's just a different kind of work. The person must be prepared to work smart, with pride in his business, and dedicate himself to maintaining our high standards of service.

- *Seasoned at sales:* Our business success hinges on being able to make the sale. A great product or service won't get referred to others if no one tries it, so we prefer someone with enough experience to know to how to nail a sale.
- *Someone who has an aptitude for management and leadership:* Franchisees run their operations. They need to make tough decisions, manage staff, and handle problems that arise. Therefore, they must have a demeanor that will earn respect from staff, clients, and vendors, and feel comfortable being in charge.
- *Dedicated to contributing ideas and building a strong relationship with the franchisor:* Our relationship with those who own our franchises is symbiotic. We welcome creative thinking, as long as we're kept in the loop and respected as having the final say on important changes.

Be aware that lots of lawsuits stem from issues related to franchises. As the franchisor, you put your brand on the line and must protect yourself by taking as many precautions as possible to bring in only people you can trust to be reliable and get the job done. You must screen franchisees even more diligently than you do employees. You also put yourself at risk legally if you make false promises or claims of grandeur that don't pan out for the franchise owner.

STARTING A FRANCHISE

Our Ten Business Commandments all apply to creating a franchise business. Follow them as a guideline for this end of your business. The following are keys for franchise success. Upon closer inspection, you'll see that these are necessary not just for the success of a franchise. They are vital to creating value for any business.

BE CREDIBLE. For a business to be successful and accepted widely, it must have credibility. To franchise or to scale your business, you must prove that you have experience at management and a winning track record, and you have to obtain media attention in local press or public recognition.

BE UNIQUE. Your business needs to be different from its competitors, both in its branding and in the service or product experience (the intangibles), to give it a marketable edge as a business opportunity and create some sort of sustainable competitive advantage. College Hunks Hauling Junk is a sizzling brand, but it wasn't until we created the client service experience that we truly captured the client loyalty we wanted. What about your business gives you a competitive advantage? Does it have both sizzle and steak? If not, develop some!

PROVIDE AN ADEQUATE RETURN. Your business must be able to generate a 15 to 20 percent return on the franchisee's investment after deducting your royalty, which is typically between 4 and 8 percent.

BE SYSTEMIZED. Your business must have systems in place and standardized operating procedures. It should be possible to teach someone to operate your business in three months or less. While franchising is an ultimate system test, being systemized also gives people or businesses the ability to operate more effectively and efficiently and to be more productive in their daily tasks.

PROVIDE ONGOING TRAINING AND SUPPORT. It's important to have a system for educating franchisees about your company and to work with them as they learn everything necessary to grow a successful business.

Research to calculate how to set the price and additional fees that a franchisee pays you. To figure out what to charge for both buying the franchise and the ongoing operation royalty fees, look at comparable businesses in the marketplace and see how they price their products or services. In many ways, franchising your business is like starting an entirely new business from scratch. You know the ins and outs of your business but must learn the ins and outs of franchising. Just as you benefit by studying businesses with concepts like the one you plan to start, it's important to study other franchisors and see what they do right and wrong. Read ads for franchises being offered. What are their terms? Then talk to a good lawyer and a good accountant who know the franchise end of business.

Typically we charge an up-front fee. As of this printing we charge $35K as a franchise fee for an exclusive zone, plus $15K for an additional exclusive territory. This will increase as our brand gains more value. Then there's an ongoing royalty, which is a percentage of total sales. Sometimes there are other fees charged for administration or sales. In return, as the franchisor, we are expected to provide certain support and improvements to the brand

and the system overall. It's a unique business partnership and relationship with expectations and obligations on both sides.

BUILDING YOUR FRANCHISE

If you plan to franchise your business, understand that it's NOT a get-rich-quick mechanism. It takes time, patience, and commitment to become successful. Since franchising depends heavily on people, you must systemize the franchise owner's functions. The more you focus on systemization, the more you'll work smarter, not harder, and the closer you'll be to becoming an effortless entrepreneur. Operating with a franchise model also makes your business more valuable to potential buyers if you decide to stop playing that particular game and start a new one.

If every aspect of a business requires one key person's involvement, the business is devalued. As we noted in chapter 4, good systems make your business run like a well-oiled machine that isn't dependent on specific people to keep it going. Your systems should be good enough to help your franchisees succeed if the systems are followed properly. While franchisees are independent business owners, many buy a franchise for the support, coaching, and consulting of the franchisor. Ongoing communication is essential.

Be the best at ONE thing.

We do weekly goal-setting and training sessions, and hold an annual conference, called our College Reunion. It's hard to teach what seems like a lifetime's worth of trial and error, but we do a weeklong Junk University training for our new franchisees. This includes going over our brand, vision, and values and starts with taking them out to learn how to haul junk, just as McDonald's teaches its franchisees how to flip hamburgers. The lessons move on to how to hire and train people to do that. Then we explain the marketing and sales end of the business, and we end with back-office administration. Basically, we teach all the systems created by learning from our mistakes. Because our company is so young, there is ongoing evolution and improvement. Manuals and checklists for every position help franchisees train their staff.

Image is everything.

We maintain the integrity of our company by focusing on our core values and enforcing brand compliance. Each franchise clearly knows what's expected of it and the importance of working with us to ensure consistent standards across the country. This is very important to enforce. Imagine if you walked into a McDonald's and asked for a Big Mac and were told they didn't sell hamburgers at that McDonald's, only fish. You'd think it was insane, and you might never eat at McDonald's again, since you wouldn't know what you'd get. Consistent service, image, and product are fundamental to franchising, allowing you to maintain a cohesive national franchise brand.

From the very beginning, have a lawyer draw up a franchise agreement that spells everything out, including what happens if a franchisee doesn't comply. We've created standards that all franchises must adhere to: uniform and logo standards, marketing material standards, sales scripting standards, client service standards, image standards, and standards for reporting to the franchisor. You can ensure that each franchise is up to par by sending secret shoppers to test them and by having site inspection checklists. If you're concerned about overseeing all your franchises, hire a national head coach who is accountable for training, coaching, and consulting with the franchisees and for enforcing the franchise agreement.

There are entire books on how to start a franchise. If you decide to make your business a franchise, consult available resources, such as the International Franchise Association (www.franchise.org), an organization with a membership including franchisors, franchisees, and suppliers. We chose to franchise our business as a cost-effective way to quickly grow our business. You have to weigh the pros and cons to decide if this is how you want to grow. If you decide it's right for you, get ready to grow your brand fast!

CHAPTER 12

SIMPLE BUSINESS, SMART MONEY
Turning Ideas You're Passionate About into Profit

The only stupid business is one you aren't passionate about. We spoke to founders of five businesses who faced a lot of skepticism about what they were doing. Each of these businesses is a labor of love. They show that if you go into an area where you have passion and knowledge, you have a real chance at success, even if outsiders might think your concept is dumb. Your idea can be funny or just an old-fashioned good concept. If you truly believe in it and can come up with a serious and credible business plan, there's no reason not to pursue it, regardless of opinions to the contrary. Chances are, if it makes you excited and passionate, it has a good shot at getting other people, particularly your target customers, excited in a way that will build buzz and create client loyalty.

The lessons from these entrepreneurs can apply to anyone. First, we'll introduce them:

REAL SOCIAL DYNAMICS (www.realsocialdynamics.com) is the world's largest international dating coaching company, according to founder Nicholas Kho. Started in 2002, the company offers live programs that provide personal coaching on how to approach and attract women. Coaches take clients to bars, clubs, and other public places to demonstrate their techniques. To date the company has trained more than twenty thousand clients in more than sixty countries. It conducts almost one thousand live programs a year. Kho says he started this company after traveling around the world meeting girls while studying social dynamics. He became really good at helping others succeed as he did.

PAWS ABOARD (www.pawsaboard.com) was founded in 2003 by Amber McCrocklin when she needed a safe way to get her hundred-pound Labrador back into her boat. She began to manufacture and distribute pet supplies. The core products are the doggy boat ladder and pet life jackets. Her company also produces floating toys and leashes, with several more products in development. The company has three employees and distributes all over the world to marine and pet companies, including PETCO, PetSmart, and West Marine. In 2008, Paws Aboard had nearly $2 million in sales of dog life jackets and ladders alone.

HAPPY BALLS (www.happyballs.com) sells soft foam antenna balls, pencil toppers, aerial balls, rearview mirror hangers, backpack hangers, and Christmas ornaments, all made of the same material and easily converted into different applications. Founded by Jeremy Turner in 2000, the company has four employees and outsources many of its manufacturing and shipping operations to reduce costs and streamline its operations. Turner says he actually enjoyed working in the corporate world but determination to be around for his kids drove him to be his own boss. His parents traveled a lot and missed his school events, and he didn't want to do that.

YoYoNation.com (yoyonation.com) is the one-stop shop for specialty yo-yos, with customers in seventy-eight countries. Founder Pat Cuartero says it's the place to get anything related to yo-yos, including bearings, parts, and accessories. When Cuartero moved to New York City and saw no yo-yo players, he wanted to connect with enthusiasts like himself and make the city a hub for yo-yo activity. So he started a business selling yo-yos. It launched in 2005 while he was still working on Wall Street. He resigned eight months later. YoYoNation.com grew rapidly and has eleven employees, four interns, and one employee in the UK. It also does corporate branding by helping people place their colors or logos on a yo-yo. The company did $1.5 million in business in its third year. Cuartero mixed technology with a simple hobby and succeeded.

Just Between Friends (www.jbfsale.com) is the leading national children's and maternity consignment event. It began between friends Shannon Wilburn and Daven Tackett. Their franchisees have two big sales events a year. Local moms and families sign up as consignors to sell items they or their children have outgrown to those who want to save money. The company has two part-time employees and a team of experts: a graphic artist, a Web developer, an event planner, and a PR company. In 1997, gross sales were $2,000. In 2008, franchise system sales reached $6.8 million, and they continue to grow rapidly. Wilburn was a teacher with young children, looking to make extra money while saving on children's items. The business began as a sale in her living room with friends and the help of Tackett. The company grew in Tulsa and is now franchised across the country.

LAUGHING TO THE BANK!

A simple idea grows by word of mouth. Even if others don't get it, if you see a market for your product or service and figure out how to reach it, you can create your own niche. When people hear our company's name, they react with the same jokes about it or the business itself. But having our brand or name elicit stupid humor is part of the genius of the brand. It creates a buzz no matter how silly or simple. Many of us successful entrepreneurs laugh our way to the bank as people scratch their heads trying to figure out how. Skepticism can be plentiful when you decide to start a business, especially one with an unusual spin.

Nicholas Kho says he took a simple idea—picking up girls—to the extreme by gathering a mastermind group of guys to teach and demonstrate how to pick up gorgeous girls. He adds, "When I first told my family about my business idea, they laughed so hard that they cried. . . . Everyone who heard about my business idea when I first started the company doubted its feasibility. In fact, some people said it was the stupidest idea they had heard in their entire life." Did it daunt him? No way! He says he had no doubt this program would be successful, since he got such amazing results from it himself. And it was! Laughing to the bank!

Jeremy Turner says friends and family still think his Happy

Balls is a silly idea and can't believe it continues to grow. His response is, "Someone has to do it! Think of all the cars that have antennas. Someone has to provide the antenna ball for them." He looked at the market, recognized the major players, and focused on a higher level of customer satisfaction, which led to increased sales and customer loyalty with a high rate of return customers. Laughing to the bank!

Daven Tackett says that when they explained their franchise system to an attorney, he asked, "Do you think this is really franchiseable?" They quickly answered, "We think we can sell these!" Shannon Wilburn says they didn't have enough business background to consider failing. They just wanted to save money. Packaging it as an event was a simple way to do that. She adds, "Most people go into businesses thinking it won't take much time and that is why businesses fail. Daven and I never thought it would become a full-time responsibility. . . . Who would have thought we could get people to volunteer at our events so they can then shop and pay us for items they buy." Laughing to the bank!

Speaking of laughing to the bank, Amber McCrocklin warns, "The bank is the number one entity that will doubt you. *Friends' and family's money* will become your most hated phrase. Don't let them get to you. That is where networking pays off the most. Your chances of finding an investor increase drastically if you network your company and yourself." She knew that no other company sold the dog ladder. Research showed her there were about ten million boats—enough to pursue the idea. Her business works because it solves a problem for many boaters who bring dogs with them. She adds, "Most people have trouble realizing that it is possible to take an idea to market and be successful." Laughing to the bank!

Pat Cuartero says he got lots of skepticism from colleagues on Wall Street when he left his six-figure job to start a yo-yo company, but he got support from yo-yo enthusiasts, who found his idea refreshing. He had a technology background and knew he could make it happen using an e-commerce approach. Cuartero believes in yo-yos, and wanted to share the joys and passions with other people. He already feels successful in the mission he set out to do. Laughing to the bank!

Find your own response to naysayers and those who discourage you from starting a business. Cuartero advises:

> Ignore anyone who doesn't believe in you. Hear what they say but don't take it to heart! Negative Nancys or Debbie Downers have no idea what they're doing with their own life and no way to make themselves feel better, so they put people down who actually try to make something of their lives. These people are sick of being stuck in a cubicle. Look at who is giving you advice and whether [it is reliable]. Take the advice of trusted advisers but stick to your vision and ignore the doubters and take the risk if it's what you truly believe in.

We remember sending a mass e-mail to friends about our new business idea and receiving smack talk about the likelihood of our success. This just added fuel to the fire. We thrive on doubt. Since we had already defined our vision, we knew it would happen. We could picture and feel what those doubters would say when our vision became reality. Naysayers can't impede your progress unless you let them.

TURNING SKEPTICAL IDEAS INTO SMART MONEY

Simple business ideas can turn into multimillion-dollar companies. Ideas that seem outlandish, implausible, or silly to most people can end up proving how smart they are in terms of financial gain. The CEOs of all the companies above began with concepts that may have sounded unlikely to make millions. Yet their businesses have all become successful. No one is too stupid to make millions. If two high school buddies can quit their day jobs and make millions by hauling junk, you can bring your own idea to fruition too! There are some common themes that these successful entrepreneurs credit their success to.

Be the best at ONE thing.

Pat Cuartero advises you to identify what your competitors are doing and how they do it. He pinpointed what was done well and what YoYoNation.com could do better. Cuartero explains:

> No one can ever be the best at everything. . . . Be the expert. The product or service for us in and of itself is a purple cow. For us to be viewed as the expert in a yo-yo, which is so simple yet we can do many difficult things, lets us stand out more

than others. Our competitors are not yo-yo players. They are
just guys selling the product, and it shows in their Web sites.

Develop staff, client, and community loyalty.

Many businesses say great customer service is critical to success. Jeremy Turner says he and his team studied the competition, pretending to be customers, to see what they did and didn't
like, adding, "We knew if we answered the phone within a few
rings, answered e-mails quickly, shipped quickly, and delivered on
promises, we would slowly win over customers." Daven Tackett
adds, "The franchisees who focus on customer service perform
at a high level. We encourage and talk about this at our train-
ings and conferences. People like feeling they are important to
your business and that you know them." Shannon Wilburn advises having high standards, since the friendliness of your staff
and volunteers can make or break your business. This keeps customers returning.

Create effective systems to keep your business on track
and enable individuals to succeed.

Wilburn says their franchise fee doubled since the beginning because "the more systems and operations we produced, the more
valuable the franchise became. Therefore, we were able to charge
more." That helped our success too. Cuartero agrees: "We've always been very technology focused. So we created an e-commerce
system and customization that is much more modern than our

competitors'. We're also overhauling it again to modernize it [further]." He advises you to be specific about how your business will operate and who your first target market is. YoYoNation. com started with enthusiasts who had the potential to become evangelists for yo-yos. It went after younger people who went to yo-yo contests and would be willing to pay.

A happy staff gives you the best chance to succeed. Jeremy Turner says, "We have people who actually love working with us because we respect them and their time." Nicholas Kho adds:

> Continually innovate. One of the core values in my company comes from the Zen philosophy: "Seek the truth from those who seek the truth. Run from those who claim to have found it." You can always learn more, and the desire for continual self-education and improvement in every aspect of your life is the core of my company. This value affects every aspect of my company culture, and the company culture will affect your customers, your mission, and everything else.

Ideas mean nothing without actions.

Take an idea that exists a step further. Amber McCrocklin says life jackets for dogs were already on the market, but customers shared what features they were unhappy with. McCrocklin modified what existed, made it cuter, and put it on the market. Sales took off! Passion about your business idea can motivate you to take action. McCrocklin wanted to make boating safer for her dogs and other people's too. Kho advises figuring out what you're passionate about: "Go online to forums and discussion groups about your passions. Read what burning questions people have and create an answer for them." Cuartero's passion for yo-yos drove him:

> While other people think yo-yos are silly, outlandish, or childish, I believe I can help convey the ideas I believe in to others where it could become part of the Olympics or X-Games one day. I feel very strongly and passionately about this, and wouldn't do the same thing I do every day if I wasn't passionate about this mission. This is how you can take something so silly and turn it into a profitable business.

Image is everything.

Branding your business and its unique qualities helps you stand out and attract customers. Cuartero says he branded the company as "the Expert of Yo-yos in the World." Kho says he branded his as the gold standard of the industry. McCrocklin says, "We have a cute logo that people really like. We attend all trade shows as well as doing co-op advertising with our customers." Turner wanted a vibrant Web presence—something that screamed his company's brand and image. He adds, "I think we were effective with the choice of our design. When someone calls us, we answer in a very friendly and welcoming tone. Our company name is Happy Balls. We try to always be HAPPY when we work with customers. Our monthly newsletter is the most effective marketing channel." Wilburn warns you to be consistent in how you brand:

Having standards that everyone follows is key. A problem in the beginning was we weren't strict on branding. To have a national appeal, we had to put in time and money in a big way. Be consistent; look for marketing material with a consistent image and feel. People should know at first glance that this is Just Between Friends and that means it is the gold standard in consignment and resale.

There are always people smarter than you—hire them!

Kho says his company invested in people and their talent. "By finding and working with amazing people, I knew that we couldn't help but be ultimately successful." Wilburn believes running a business takes more time and talent than you probably realize. She explains, "One key to success is surrounding yourself with smart people. You don't have to be an expert at everything. I thought many times, I have no idea how to do this stuff, but quickly learned how to find people who did know. As tasks, problems, and decisions come, surround yourself with people who can help you get the answers and solutions."

Mistakes are problems only if you do not learn from them.

You *will* make mistakes when you begin, and then more later. Cuartero says business school doesn't teach many things that are needed to be successful, so he and his partner dove in headfirst, wanting to do something challenging. Things arose that they had no idea would come up. But he loved it, since every day was a new experience, unlike a corporate job, which becomes dull quickly.

He adds, "I myself was the biggest obstacle. I learned every step of the way. You kinda learn [how to handle mistakes] as you go along."

These entrepreneurs learned from their mistakes and it helped them grow. Kho says that to get his company off the ground, he acquired a $5 million mansion in the Hollywood Hills and rented it to business associates, who were also his best friends. This created a roadblock, since they lived and worked together. Their entire lives revolved around one another. Eventually, they had to work out many personal and professional conflicts stemming from strong personalities and large egos. He adds, "I learned I need to separate the personal and professional boundaries of my relationships."

Turner also learned a valuable lesson when first starting:

We spent $7,000 on small brochures to hand out at a trade show. It was $7,000 we didn't have. We thought it would make our presentation better and sell more product. We made it so cute. People who didn't want to buy the product picked up our brochure because it looked good and said, "Happy Balls." They showed their friends and then tossed them. Each brochure [cost] $2.75. We sold less product at that trade show than at the next one with black-and-white photocopies.

Our business evolved slowly. The only lightning bolt that hit our company was the name, College Hunks Hauling Junk. We knew it was marketable after we put out flyers and our phone started ringing. But even when Omar won the business-plan competition, we still didn't consider launching the business. We got jobs and began to hate life. Then we remembered that when we started, we knew little about business and were a ragtag operation. Slowly it sunk in that if we could make money doing nothing right, imagine what we could do if we learned from our mistakes. And we did.

DEVELOPING A SMART NICHE

This is a great time to start a business. Nicholas Kho says niche businesses continually start up because there are so many untapped needs and wants of consumers. Amber McCrocklin thinks people are getting more creative and realize there are avenues now that allow you to sell your ideas. The Internet makes promotion much easier. "Starting a Web site with a shopping cart is a great way to start a business, realize if there is any interest, and sell your product at full retail—realizing higher margins," says McCrocklin. Pat Cuartero agrees it's a good time because technology is accessible, labor and resources are less expensive, and you can negotiate with vendors and outsource technology, design, and PR. He says you have a lot more leverage these days.

Start with a vision, create a strategic plan, and live by it.

Daven Tackett advises providing customers with a wow factor— something that sets you apart. She says, "Our wow factor at JBF is we have so much stuff in one place and it is high-quality merchandise at very low prices. When they walk in, they can hardly tell if something has been used, and they are impressed." Wilburn agrees. "Set yourself apart. People will go to the one that is most convenient *and* does the best job. Do the work, put time and effort into it, and do the best. It will succeed." Cuartero says that if people see what you're doing is better than others, they'll become believers.

Jeremy Turner says money is a big factor. "The most important component of running a business is not your product, not your business cards, not your T-shirts, but your cash flow." McCrocklin recommends doing your research to make sure there's a big enough market potential to make your investment worth it, adding:

> Pricing is very important. Work with an expert in the industry to help you set your retail price. *Boater's World* helped me when I first presented the ladder to them. They were very instrumental in my success. Continue to work on your suppliers to get your costs down. Use free PR to your benefit. Send out press releases to all local, national, and industry publications about your new super-duper company. . . . Industry trade shows are a great way to get started. Go slowly. The first one, just walk. Do not get a booth. Make sure the show is a good fit and is well attended before you invest your time and precious cash. Put a small ad in the back of a trade magazine to see what kind of response you get. Ask others in the profession their opinion.

Develop staff, client, and community loyalty.

Wilburn recommends playing to your and your business partner's and/or coworkers' strengths. She and Tackett have very
distinct personality and business styles but worked to mesh them.
They both believe in giving back to the community. Each franchise partners with a local charity and donates items and sometimes cash during each event. That's a passion for them. Cuartero
was a semiprofessional yo-yo player in high school. He used his
passion for yo-yoing to start his business, and says, "Niche stems
from passion and enthusiasm."

Tackett advises:

> Strive to have a varied target market and advertising plan.
> You need to know how to market your business and get the
> word out there. Start small and build. We did not expect that
> we would have to start at the bottom and work our way up,
> but we did. You get to increase your advertising and mar-
> keting as you have income and resources to increase [it].
> Everyone wants everything right now. We didn't operate
> that way.

Amber McCrocklin's mantra has always been "Failure is not
an option." She chanted it for the first four years. "The power of
positive thinking is huge. Now I think expansion, big, growth,
millions. Large words keep me moving forward."

Cuartero emphasizes that you can't be afraid to take risks,
which are part of being an entrepreneur. He warns:

If you're not willing to take those risks, then you can't call yourself an entrepreneur. Being in a cushy Wall Street job can make you risk averse, but being an entrepreneur, there is no way you can move forward without taking risks, and if you fail, so what? You just get back on the horse and start again. Your risks need to feel right in your gut. Be smart in taking your risks, and KEEP MOVING FORWARD. Don't be stagnant. Otherwise new competitors will take your market share. It becomes part of your life. If you don't continue to nurture it like an infant, then it will die off. Keep innovating.

A common misconception is that if there are already many businesses servicing a certain niche, there's no room for another one. This is simply NOT TRUE. No matter how tiny the niche, you'll typically find multiple businesses offering the exact same products or services. It's not what your business is that's important, but what level you can take it to. Imagine a small pond with ten fish, from small to huge, that all feed off the same algae. The biggest grew because it was quicker. As it grew it consumed more food. The smaller fish feed off scraps the larger ones miss. Another fish enters the pond—the tiniest of them all. It can't compete in quickness or size but discovers lots of algae under pebbles at the bottom. It learns to maneuver under and around the pebbles better than the others. Over time the tiny fish becomes one of the biggest fish in the pond.

That tiny fish is your business, the algae are your customers, the pond is your niche, and the other fish are your competitors. Some fish are big only because they were first in the pond.

They don't necessarily have a special skill for getting food (finding customers). They grew and rely on size to bully other fish. Some competitors are big only because they were first to offer that particular product or service. But remember, bigger fish require more food to stay alive just as bigger businesses have higher overhead, salaries, and the like. The tiny fish found an X factor when it targeted algae under the pebbles.

The College Hunks Hauling Junk X factor is our brand name and marketing ability. We were a small lean business that didn't require lots of money (algae) to stay alive. We leveraged this to grow rapidly and take over market share (the pond). Remember that revenue is vanity, profit is sanity, and cash flow is king. This means that increasing sales shouldn't be the only focus of your business. You must also properly manage your expenditures. Since smaller fish initially have less access to food (sales), they must also be aware of how many calories (cash) they burn and how much they store in reserve if they don't eat (make another sale) for a while.

Find an industry that interests you and try to create the most targeted niche you can think of, as these entrepreneurs did. If you want a boxing gym, start one that caters to a very targeted segment, like senior citizens. It could offer a fun and exciting way for them to get in shape. Now you can target senior citizen homes and senior newspapers. The beauty is that no senior citizen would ever dream of stepping into a boxing gym, but if you customize the gym for them, you'll create a brand-new market of customers that never existed, just as the tiny fish found algae in a place where none of the other fish looked for it. So can you! We have a few final words from these entrepreneurs:

Pat Cuartero: Get your accounting and legal systems in place at the very beginning so you're not behind when you grow. It's a huge headache, but if you get the processes nailed in the beginning it will be better going forward.

Amber McCrocklin: Start small and have patience. Starting a business is very expensive. I had a high-paying job that I kept for the first year while I launched my business. Networking is also a big part of being successful. The more one travels, attends social functions, business meetings, etc., the more contacts one retains and the more opportunities come one's way.

Jeremy Turner: Work for "the man" as long as you can. Start your business on the side, after work, on weekends and holidays. Work at a "real job" to save money, get health care, and have a secure source of cash. Let your business run on its profits for as long as you can without taking a paycheck. Use your real job as your income, but pump all the money from your venture back into the business until it can sustain itself. Build up six months' worth of cash for your company before you quit your job.

Nicholas Kho: Make sure that you have clear expectations between you and everyone you work with because nothing is more important than avoiding any possible social or professional violations of expectations. Having everything in writing in advance will clarify and prevent millions of potential problems that may erupt in the future.

Shannon Wilburn: Surround yourself with smart people. Start by researching to find out whom the best people are to consult and work with. When you have an idea or a plan, write it down, set goals, and revisit them. Post them where you can see them and be reminded to do them.

* * *

The entrepreneurs featured in this chapter are examples of the many thousands of people who had a dream and chose to pursue it. We're not saying that it's easy to start a business and make it successful. People will doubt you. You may doubt yourself. But it can be done if you're passionate enough about your vision and willing to do the work to make it happen. Choose: continue dreaming while you stay in your day job, or start the game of entrepreneurship. You can, if the passion, vision, and follow-through are in you. Join us!

CHAPTER 13

KEEPING YOUR EDGE
Working Smarter and Playing Harder

ere we were, two young, hungry businessmen, riding to an important meeting in a landscape truck. We were meeting with top TV executives to pitch our latest and greatest reality TV show concept about College Hunks Hauling Junk. Knowing they had agreed to meet with us was remarkable. We flew across the country the night before to get a good night's sleep and make sure we arrived on time—all for a one-hour meeting! Our friend Frenchy drove us to the meeting an hour early, so we killed time by going up a long, winding road to a lookout point. When it was time to head back down—problem! The car wouldn't start. It was time to put our troubleshooting skills to work.

We suggested rolling the car down the hill, but it couldn't be shifted into neutral with the engine off. Frenchy's battery jump starter didn't work either. It felt like we were in a sitcom. Nick had a torn ACL and, in a giant brace and carrying crutches, was practically immobile. We were close to panicking. Finally, we flagged down a landscape truck and scored a ride down. We sat in our freshly dry-cleaned suits on the back ledge of the pickup truck, behind a bed filled with shovels and mulch, determined to make our meeting. It felt reminiscent of George and Jerry going to pitch a show about nothing in a *Seinfeld* episode. We took it as a sign. We'd begun our business in a truck with lots of junk, so this was a good omen. We went to the meeting about our new TV show pumped!

BALANCING WORK AND PLAY

Success is sweet, that's for sure. After working very hard to launch a business and then building it, seeing your company's profit increasing, your staff growing, and the reach of the goods or services you market expanding can allow you to take a big deep breath. That's when you've truly become an effortless entrepreneur. But the respite can last too long if complacency starts to influence your activities. You must not take your business for granted; stay on your game and continue to work on building it. Of course, you should allow yourself to have fun. As you delegate more responsibility, you can make more time for fun. We did. But it's important to make sure you keep a balance between work and play.

Nick suggested moving to Tampa after we sold our first franchises. It got extremely difficult to hire reliable people to answer phones in the D.C. area. We also needed a new adventure. So we moved. There was no state income tax in Florida, and real estate was cheap. Tampa was an outstanding call center city—and full of beautiful women! The cost of living was much cheaper, so we could pay low- and midlevel people much less and still attract great executives, since our pay was consistent with that in other cities.

The birthplace of our company was Florida, so Tampa fit our company culture and brand. It is a young and colorful city, less conservative than many, which is what our culture is about. Living there has been a blast. Our location is near the beach and we bought a boat. While we intend to play harder, it's important to work smarter than ever too. We continue to work ON our business to expand and have more fun than ever. Getting that balance makes us happy guys!

When we moved, our mentor Bill Hefner advised, "Don't get fat and lazy." It's easy to get complacent and overconfident after some success. You can lose sight of your overall vision or want a break from the game. We were susceptible to this: we were twenty-five years old, with a boat and two luxury cars, and living in the most beautiful mansion imaginable. We started losing focus on our business as we became more enamored of the glamour of being young and rich. It's natural to celebrate and chill out after working hard to build a business. Once you've implemented systems to automate it, you can step back from day-to-day operations and continue to reap the benefits—the process becomes nearly effortless. Our business was essentially on cruise control. That's good in a strong economy, but when it's weak, storms come fast and hard, which is why no matter how effortless it may seem, you should never become complacent.

Imagine taking your hands off the steering wheel of a boat in the middle of the ocean. If your boat is twenty feet long and has only a few passengers, it may ride straight for a little while, but even the smallest wave can knock it off course. The bigger you build your business, the larger your boat becomes. You can put it on autopilot for longer periods. But remember, even the *Titanic* sank when it hit an iceberg, so you can never become overconfident about what you've built. When we took our hands off the wheel, sales decreased by 30 percent, trucks in the D.C. operation began to fall apart, the logos were all scratched up, and employee morale got low. The systems couldn't withstand the rigors of time and the economic challenges without us being there to oversee them. It was a costly but valuable lesson.

Thousands of businesses went under in the blink of an eye in 2008. Their owners weren't prepared to pilot the ship. The economy and markets are an undulating, ever-changing sea. You can't leave your ship on autopilot forever. Someone must navigate. When a business drifts off course, ways must be found to spend less and sell more. While your goal may be to systemize your business enough to leave for a year, that's not likely to happen. Always be alert to market conditions, new competitors, and innovations, which continually evolve. It's critical to remain dynamic and ready to handle turbulence.

We keep at least one hand on the steering wheel of our business at all times, using good advice from ESPN *SportsCenter* anchor Scott Van Pelt, who told us to "stay humble, stay hungry." The most successful entrepreneurs are driven and aren't swayed by overconfidence or feeling invincible. Don't buy into the hype of your success. The 2009 economy showed that "Don't get fat and lazy" always rings true, no matter what level of the game you reach. Keep playing it to the fullest. Of course, take vacations and take time off to party. Your personal life is as important as your company. Leave the business mentality for a while. But have a system for that. Having a partner makes it easier because you can share watch duty.

Never sacrifice health, family,
or friendships for business reasons.

President Barack Obama said, "Focusing your life solely on making a buck shows a certain poverty of ambition. It asks too little of yourself. Because it's only when you hitch your wagon to something larger than yourself that you realize your true potential." To have true success in business and in life you must excel in seven areas: self, loving family relationships, work, health, money, spirituality, fun. Make good health a priority. Working too hard causes health problems and leads to burnout, which leads to mistakes and injury. Doing too little with your business can lead to boredom, which is equally bad. If you don't find a balance, you'll burn out physically, mentally, or both. That interferes with building a successful business.

KEEPING YOURSELF MOTIVATED

If you find yourself succumbing to the good life created by business success, or getting complacent or starting to lose interest, motivate yourself by setting higher goals. A business constantly evolves. Your future goals and vision should guide you. Dynamic action and leadership are the recipe for success in an ever-changing marketplace. Raise your vision and goals higher. If your target is in dollars, double it! What's the worst that can happen? If we fail tomorrow, we'll come back and make ten times more than the first time. That's a renegade entrepreneur's mentality!

Start with a vision, create a strategic plan, and live by it.

Never think you know it all. There's so much useful information you can tap into to stimulate your spirit to go higher with your business, and there are amazing people to learn from. We read business books and attend conferences and workshops for entrepreneurs as much as possible. A professional athlete doesn't make the big leagues and then stop practicing. There's a big difference between a Kobe Bryant and a bench player. Just because you make the big show doesn't mean you'll stay great. You must continually hone your craft. All the knowledge we accumulate pushes us to grow our business further.

Our interest in continuing to build our business remains strong because our vision is so clear that we can taste it, feel it, smell it, and see it. When that vision starts to become a reality, it's hard not to be interested in taking it to a higher level. We love using sports and video game analogies because they add an extra level of fun to the game. We look at ourselves as minor-league players who are close to making it into the big leagues. We know exactly how it will feel and look once we make it, so it's not just a job. There's an emotional connection to working hard. If your soul isn't in it, your body will only half-ass it. In that case, you might want to revamp your goals. But if you love your business, think about it as your baby and raise it well, even if it gives you some problems or seems not to need your help anymore. If you love it, keep growing it.

We pay attention to each small success, and each one motivates us. Don't focus on just long-term goals, which may take years to accomplish. If you're attached only to those, you'll miss celebrating minivictories. The magic is in moments that made us successful—the goose-bump moments, those small experiences that showed we were on the right track, milestones that made us think, Holy crap, this might actually work! Goose-bump moments are when your passion comes to life: you get a warm feeling, and the hair on the back of your neck stands up. Such moments are the purpose of your business, your reason for getting up each day.

Our goose-bump moments come when we see the lives we've touched and the doors we've opened throughout our journey. When a client excitedly recounts her enjoyable experience with our company, we get goose bumps. When an employee clearly buys into our vision and comes up with a fantastic idea, we get goose bumps. When we see our trucks in other cities, we get goose bumps. When we see pegs on the map showing cities we're in, we get goose bumps. Pay attention to your goose-bump moments for motivation!

THE LAW OF ATTRACTION MAKES THINGS HAPPEN

Everything that's happened to us has been a result of our consciously visualizing what we want. Our business success, book, media attention, boat, cars, and move to sunny Florida—all have resulted from our thoughts and ideas. You have the power to control yours! What happens to you is a direct result of past thoughts.

What will happen is based wholly on what you currently think. From the very beginning, we knew we wouldn't be junk slingers and had a vision and a game plan for where to go. This enabled us to succeed much faster than anyone could imagine—except ourselves. Even when no one believes in your business vision, continue to visualize it and know it will happen, and you'll have a good shot!

Ideas mean nothing without actions.

The Law of Attraction supports your thoughts. You attract what you intend to get. We put our intentions in writing when we spelled out our vision and held fast to the intention of making it all a reality. Visualize your future business, get excited about it, make a plan of action to build it, and believe it will come to fruition. You'll never be a success if you don't believe you already are. It's important to have a twenty- to twenty-five-year long-term vision, a three- to five-year goal, and a one-year plan. All decisions and actions will stem from these. With this in mind, we wrote our vision for the future that's in chapter 4. We encourage you to do the same. Review it monthly and see it happening! Our big goal is to "haul anything from anywhere at any time." Visualizing our trucks dispatching at any time to any place is exciting, motivating, and imaginative.

When you focus on your vision, your intentions can manifest it if you think, feel, and see it happening. There will be times along the way when you have doubts. Try your best to move past them by reading your vision plan until it grounds you. When you focus your thoughts on your intentions for your business and your actions on working to make them real, you can override fears and doubts. We've allowed doubt to rear its ugly head when things didn't work out easily. There are days when we think that it's all too hard, it's not going to work, and we'll just be another flash in the pan. But those doubts are self-fulfilling if you allow them to permeate your thought process. You have to cast them out and truly believe in your ability to make it happen. Then it can!

NINE WAYS TO STAY STRONG
IN ANY ECONOMY—COLLEGE HUNKS STYLE

Economic downturns and recessions happen. A successful business is prepared to roll with any economy. When the recession began in 2008, our business was three years old and growing steadily. Money became tight and people thought twice about having their homes or offices cleaned out using a service like ours. We're not the cheapest. Discretionary consumers cut back. But did this stop our growth? NO WAY! We found ways to work with the recession instead of thinking, Woe is me. You can keep your business solvent in any economy if you get creative, keep your eye on your goals, and don't let a dip in the economy scare you. Here are lessons that worked for us:

1. **Set bold and aggressive long-term goals and create short-term internal competitions.** Even with economic setbacks, having a long-term goal in place motivates and keeps the team focused on the big picture, not just tomorrow. Our internal competitions (discussed in chapter 6) got even more

important for generating team loyalty and a loyal client database when the economy slumped.

2. Share as much information as possible. It was extremely important to share information—sales, Web traffic, call volume, key profit—with our team, especially when the economy got worse. This alerted them to the decline in the number of jobs and average job size. Front-line team members let the clients' price sensitivity dictate their bid prices, driving down our pricing. Since we NEVER want to sacrifice our pricing integrity, they had to make a conscious effort to get our average job size back up to par. If we hadn't shared these metrics, they'd have simply blamed the decrease in sales on the economy.

3. Stay positive and reiterate your core values as much as possible. College Hunks Hauling Junk has four core values:

- Build leaders.
- Create a fun, enthusiastic team environment.
- Always brand.
- Listen to, fulfill, and delight our team, franchisees, and clients.

By reiterating these and remaining positive, we've led our team through the rough waters of the economic storm.

4. Celebrate achievements. It's crucial to celebrate achievements and recognize team members. We write about specific

individuals and do employee and franchisee spotlights on our
public blog. Our rewards are more symbolic since they often
cost little, yet are great fun. Once the celebration for hitting a
goal was simply a jumping high five, since we had no budget for
a big reward. Everyone laughed, but athletes do it when they
score a touchdown, so it seemed like a fun way to recognize an
accomplishment. When we didn't hit our goal but came close, we
did a sitting high five during our staff meeting as a consolation.

5. **Say "yes" more by finding ways to accommodate requests,
but know when to say "no."** It's helpful to say "yes" to team
requests in order to boost morale, but it's also important to say
"no." Time is your most valuable asset. When we began, we
were flattered when people vied for our attention. In reality, they
just drained our energy, and sometimes our money. We learned
to say "no." Balance saying "yes" and turning people down. During an economic downturn, saying "yes" to your team goes a
long way toward maintaining morale. But say "no" to things
that drain your valuable time.

6. **Get close to clients through multiple channels and
touch points.** We have several mechanisms for measuring client loyalty. We do follow-up calls, called "happy checks," to
confirm satisfaction, and use an e-mail survey with incentives
to respond, like a $25 restaurant gift certificate (it costs us $7).
Systems measure repeat and referral business. We maintain
Telephone Tuesdays and Thank-You Thursdays. Emphasiz-
ing our team member profile cards and vote cards is essential

because those individuals are the ones clients see most. Without their connection to clients, there would be no future for the business.

7. **Facilitate roundtable and strategic discussions across departments.** We began an optional monthly phone conference with five franchise owners that focused on pushing measurable growth. They discussed best practices, held one another accountable, facilitated meetings, and controlled the agenda. To avoid a bitchfest—just complaints about corporate—we spelled out a code of conduct to focus only on growing sales.

8. **Lead by example from a corporate standpoint by leveraging low-cost technology and strategies.** We invested in improving our Web site, software, and marketing strategies during the downturn so our team knew we were still pushing forward. We hired a University of South Florida PR class to find out why we generated great national press but got little local coverage in franchisee markets. The students created a two-hundred-page report with market research, client data, media lists, localized press releases, webinars to teach franchisees how to use releases locally, and other recommendations. It would have cost $100,000 if we'd hired a consulting company, but we paid $500 for the end-of-year presentation to the professor! We also hired a videographer found on Craigslist to get videos on YouTube and a PR intern to blog and increase our social network presence.

9. **Have consistent communication.** Daily huddles, weekly and monthly meetings, and quarterly strategy sessions are more important during trying times. Create a meeting rhythm, as discussed earlier.

WORKING SMARTER, PLAYING HARDER, AND MAKING IT ALL "EFFORTLESS"

Time is our most precious commodity. Being able to choose how to spend yours is the ultimate freedom. An entrepreneur can have even less "me" time than someone with a day job. But it doesn't matter if you're passionate about what you do. We don't go to work; we go to play. Life is pleasurable, even with long hours devoted to our business. We're passionate about playing the game and get as much personal satisfaction and pleasure as we do from playing tennis. However, the most important rule of the game is: Never let it control your life. Always stay in control. If the game controls you, it becomes an obsession that harms your health, relationships, and life. As business gets complicated or the game has bigger challenges, the hamsters in your head run faster and wake you up at night. That's working harder, not smarter. Life can quickly spin out of control.

We like to socialize. At first we worked and played hard, and we would have burned out if we hadn't learned to create systems to maintain the business without continual effort or attention from one of us. When Nick went on vacation our first year, he constantly checked e-mails and made business calls, since his responsibilities were still directly tied to daily productivity. After implementing systems, we went white-water rafting for a long weekend with our phones off. That was true freedom! We enjoyed ourselves and the business functioned well. In our absence it actually hit record sales.

Businesses must grow to survive. If you reach a certain level and choose to just keep it steady, you're simply employed by yourself, and you may eventually burn out or grow bored from lack of personal or professional growth. A product business is more easily systemized and outsourced. It's extremely difficult to remove yourself entirely from a service business. You can hire a CEO but must still meet occasionally. Once you're successful, competitors will claw to surpass you. Whoever provides the best client service wins. Smaller competitors can easily outflank a fat and lazy giant.

Create effective systems to keep your business on track and enable individuals to succeed.

It's your choice. Work harder to stimulate growth, which depletes your freedom, or enjoy the challenge of the game by systemizing your position and motivating team members to systemize theirs, which will make it easier to run your business effortlessly. People love a job when it's fun, stimulating, and challenging. It's work when it takes time from what you'd rather do. When we started, we loved every minute. It was new and exciting. Then it began to seem like a chore or burden hanging over us. We had to either quit or embrace the challenge as a new game level. If we hadn't made it a game, we'd have burned out by now.

Many lifelong entrepreneurs say they'll never retire, since work is their fun. George Naddaff, founder of Boston Market, left retirement at eighty years old to launch a new concept during a terrible economy. He's wealthy beyond imagination yet chooses to roll the dice one more time and goes to the office every day to help grow his start-up. We met billionaire Fred DeLuca, founder of Subway. His original goal was to have 1,000 locations. His wife thought he was crazy. Now there are more than 31,000. There was no reason for him to be at the International Franchise Association convention, yet he was there, still playing the game and looking for new concepts to roll out.

Be willing to play the game passionately. It starts by stepping onto the playing field and committing to playing the game hard. Our goal with this book is to inspire and help lead an entrepreneurial movement for those who choose to play. We want to help you avoid getting kicked in the head if you join this adventure, and to change the lives of those willing to believe in the potential of entrepreneurship. We tell our story so you can connect with ideas and learn from our experiences. We're challenging the status quo. Instead of going through the daily motions of fitting in, following instructions, and keeping our head down, we chose another way to earn a living.

Entrepreneur's mantra: Maintain control, stay focused, and react quickly.

Entrepreneurs founded the country. They'll continue taking it to new heights. More people than ever are interested in the American Dream of business ownership; the trend is stronger in an unstable economy. By mapping out what's next in business, work, family, or life, you have a road map and a destination. Enjoy the journey! We use the analogy of driving cross-country at night. Your headlights show what's just ahead. Yet you can still follow the road as it twists and turns. If you don't have a destination you'll just drive aimlessly. Without a road map you'll get lost. When you create your vision plan, you can follow it, step by step, to build the business of your dreams.

The best time to start a business is RIGHT NOW. You'll never have less responsibility than you do at this exact instant. Tomorrow you'll have more responsibilities, next year even more responsibilities. Responsibilities create excuses for why you can't start a business. That's why it's so viable to launch a business at a young age. Students are accustomed to living modestly. They don't have a mortgage and typically don't have kids. If you're just getting started, a business failure won't set you further back than you were at graduation. But no matter what your age, if starting a business calls you, answer with passion!

You don't have to quit your job, but at least read about starting your own business. If you get as much of an adrenaline rush as we did about catching a dream, you might try. There's significant opportunity for those with an eye for it, who can define their vision. We have lofty goals. Everyone who works at our company is juiced about the vision of building something much larger as a group than a single individual could do on his own. If it wasn't College Hunks Hauling Junk, we'd start another business. The truth is we can't see ourselves working for someone else. That's not an option. We plan to have more businesses, more investments, and more success. And the best part is that by working smarter, not harder, we've made it easy to focus on what is fun and stimulates us, without having to devote effort to the daily grind.

A FEW FINAL WORDS

Nick: I struggled with self-doubt and didn't know what to do with my life after entering the "real world," thinking I'd climb the corporate ladder. But I was extremely disillusioned, with no direction or guidance. I told my mom I wanted to use my people skills and do something more dynamic than sitting in a cubicle. She joked that I could be a receptionist. I felt empty. It seemed like everything I'd ever done or looked forward to as a child had been crushed into a six-by-six cubicle. Once we started our business, I was reenergized, yet still had moments of despair about how to grow it to the level I envisioned. I had created the vision but not the steps to turn it into a reality.

It felt hopeless. I couldn't go through life as I'd pictured it, and I don't want you to go through that. It wasn't until we began to explore and learn about paths traveled by other successful entrepreneurs that the steps became clearer and the journey more enjoyable. It's my vision and goal to inspire would-be entrepreneurs to get out of the stands as spectators and join us on the entrepreneurial playing field as participants, without getting kicked. And I want to help support those entrepreneurs who've already taken that big first leap of faith and are on their way in pursuit of their vision.

*   *   *

Omar: When I walk into a high school or college classroom to speak, I look out at the young men and women staring back at me. I was just like many of them growing up. I didn't know what I wanted to do or where I'd end up. Sometimes I didn't even care. Most people want to try something different and live a life that's exciting. The main point I try to make is that if I can do this, anybody can! My life didn't change for the better after I started making money or after College Hunks Hauling Junk became a national company.

My life changed for the better the first day I set out on my own with a beat-up cargo van and realized I could make money on my own terms and setting my own rules. If we had started this business and it had failed miserably, I would have learned, grown, and had just as much fun doing it. That would have made my attempt successful. There's no better time than now to try something new. Some businesses won't get off the ground and some will. If you fail, dust yourself off and try again. When you succeed, stay humble. Either way, hang on tight because you are riding the American Dream.

Thank you for taking the time to read our book. We hope you'll share your thoughts, experiences, and inspirations with us.
nick@effortlessentrepreneur.com
omar@effortlessentrepreneur.com

ACKNOWLEDGMENTS

Nick: This book turned into a reality as a result of the support and guidance of several people. In particular, thanks to my mom and dad for their unwavering support of my entrepreneurial exploits as an adult, their tolerance and steadfastness in dealing with my irresponsible and reckless behavior while growing up, and for instilling in me a level of self-confidence that has helped me feel like I can accomplish anything and rise above any obstacles. Thanks to my sister for her inspirational and worldly accomplishments and for always taking time to proofread my papers during high school and college, and also for taking the time to read our book manuscript before we even had a publisher.

Thanks to Daylle Deanna Schwartz for helping us turn our scatterbrained thoughts into a well-crafted, well-organized book, and for putting up with our stubborn personalities throughout the process. Thanks to Daylle for introducing us to our agent, Linda Konner, and thanks to Linda for putting forth such a valiant effort to get us signed by such an amazing publishing company. Thanks to the Crown Publishing Group at Random House for believing in our vision, and thanks to our editor, Nathan Roberson, for sharing in our vision and helping develop it into a reality.

Thanks to the College Hunks Hauling Junk family (team members, clients, and franchise owners). By contributing and committing yourself to making our vision part of your own, you have built an incredible, powerful, and revered national brand that is a part of you and is the backbone and inspiration for this book. Thanks to my extended family and colleagues who gave us positive feedback throughout the evolution of our business and the writing of this book.

Thanks to my true friends for being like a second family. Thanks to my girlfriends of past, present, and future for putting up with my obsessive-compulsive behavior and believing in me, if even for a fleeting moment.

Thanks to the teachers who wrote me off and said I would amount to nothing. You motivated me to prove you wrong. Thanks to the teachers and counselors who believed in me and said I was something special. You gave me the confidence and the knowledge to prove you right.

Thanks to my basketball coaches, especially Bobby Fields, for helping me realize that I could make up for my lack of talent by focusing my energy and developing an unwavering drive, dedication, and passion to succeed.

Thanks to every entrepreneur and author who has proven that it is possible for ordinary people to create extraordinary value.

Last, but not least, thanks to my business partner and best friend, Omar Soliman, for being the visionary and creative leader in our organization and for coming up with the idea to write *Effortless Entrepreneur* and for having the dedication to turn it into a reality.

Omar: I want to thank the people who fueled my passion the most, starting with Lynn Skynear and Moustafa Soliman. I know you as Mom and Dad but you are the two most influential people in my life. I don't believe in luck, but I feel lucky to be your son. Mom, it was your van that started this business and the summers working in your furniture store that taught me why small business is so important for this country. Dad, being able to talk to you and hear your stories about everything from business to girls made me the man I am today.

Thanks to the rest of my family, aka, my fan-base, from Grandma to my uncles, aunts, and cousins for always cheering me on. I would like to thank my close group of friends—many of whom I grew up with in D.C.—for all the great times and laughs.

I also have to thank the University of Miami. As a kid who grew up hating school, authority, and anything classroom-related, it is hard to believe that I am so beholden to an academic institution. I truly would not be where I am today if it was not for the opportunity the University of Miami gave me through The Rothschild Entrepreneurship Competition. How many colleges hand out $36,000+ in prize money for business plan competitions every year?

I knew Nick was the right business partner a few months before we even started the business. He was asked by a big nightclub promotions company to help promote a failing night at one of their biggest venues. When I drove by the club there was a line around the block. My mouth dropped open even wider when I walked in and the place was completely packed. I grabbed Nick and asked how he pulled it off. Rather than go the same route every promoter takes, he said he contacted the alumni department of the local high schools and had them advertise the event to their contact list as an alumni get-together. The club's owner wanted to fire the promotions company on the spot and hire Nick in its place! A true leader, working smart and playing hard.

INDEX